Shanker A. Singham is the top conservative economist of his generation. In his latest book, he explains how market distortions affect trade, domestic regulation and economic growth globally. This new work represents Singham's most compelling effort to illustrate the scope and depth of regulatory overreach with new metrics. I urge policymakers to use these provocative new insights to drive game-changing impact in their countries' economies, poverty alleviation and human flourishing worldwide. The numbers now prove what Singham has long said intuitively – that the upside of restrained and thoughtful regulation is massive, but the cost of getting regulation wrong is – and always has been – catastrophic, leading us into a potentially very dangerous and polarized world.

– **Kerry Healey,** *Former Lt-Governor, Massachusetts and former President, Babson College*

The US trade system regulating imports is in need of a remedy that is flexible enough to address the wide range of non-market practices in the global economy that damage US firms and workers. Shanker A. Singham has been ahead of his time in developing this proposal to quantify and redress market distortions that damage trade and competition. This timely book will be highly useful for policymakers who are navigating the challenging trade world we face today. It is a must-read for anyone who worries about declining productivity and economic growth in Western nations and around the world

– **Meredith Broadbent**, *Former Chairman of International Trade Commission. Former Assistant USTR for Industry, Market Access and Telecommunications*

Shanker A. Singham has been the global leader in studying – and measuring – how government-imposed economic market distortions (ACMDs) distort trade, harm competition and weaken property rights. These effects combine to significantly reduce economic growth around the world.

In addition to authoring path-breaking studies of ACMDs, he chairs the non-partisan Growth Commission. The Commission is an independent organisation of international economists producing new research and dynamic economic modelling which identifies policies that can increase income per person.

This book represents Singham's latest and most important effort to establish and refine metrics that estimate the economic harm stemming from ACMDs.

The numbers now prove what Singham has been saying intuitively – eliminating ACMDs has a tremendous economic upside. It spurs economic growth and raises per capita GDP for all citizens.

Public policymakers would do well to take note of Singham's findings. Future global economic prosperity may depend upon governments' willingness to root out and tackle ACMDs.

– **Alden Abbott,** *Senior Research Fellow, Mercatus Center at George Mason University, former General Counsel, Federal Trade Commission.*

Channelling the 17th-century philosopher Thomas Hobbes, Shanker A. Singham writes, "The normal state of human beings is poverty and war". Singham then spends the next 123 pages of his new book on anti-competitive market distortions outlining how countries, by abandoning government-imposed restrictions, can (and should) enhance national prosperity and, ultimately, peace. Singham's insightful and timely book ought to be required reading for federal policymakers".

– **James Carter,** *Former Associate Director, National Economic Council, The White House*

Written by one of the world's greatest economic thinkers, this book illustrates the scale of market distortions in the global economy. Shanker A. Singham expertly weaves the scale of distortion into the wider economic and national security picture, precisely describing how the world will be more at risk of conflict and war if these distortions are not dealt with. The world grows more dangerous by the moment, and Shanker A. Singham presents a way out of poverty and war into prosperity and peace. It is a must read.

– **John Poindexter**, *Former National Security Advisor*

International Trade, Regulation and the Global Economy

The barriers between the voluntary exchange of willing buyers and willing sellers have progressively been reduced through trade liberalisation, competition and better property rights protection. However, the world has done significantly less well in reducing barriers involving competition and property rights. This book analyses how the economic prosperity which was promised has been undermined by these "Anti-Competitive Market Distortions", which damage international trade as well as domestic conditions of competition and, ultimately, GDP per capita.

This book first describes the nature of the Anti-Competitive Market Distortions problem and how it has impacted countries since the 1990s. It also highlights a gap in policymaking, detailing how Anti-Competitive Market Distortions have existed in an ungoverned space in both international trade and competition theory. The book also explores the various models of the impact of Anti-Competitive Market Distortions, including the original econometric model to measure the quantum of distortion – and three new variations on this – as well as an agency-based Model. Finally, drawing on techniques from probabilistic methods and quantum mechanics, the book examines the possibility of a probabilistic model to assess the real impact of Anti-Competitive Market Distortions on GDP per capita growth around the world in a far more dynamic and real-time sense than has been possible thus far.

This book will be invaluable to academics and students of trade, competition and international relations in both the legal and economic disciplines.

Shanker A. Singham is one of the world's leading international trade and competition lawyers/economists. He is the CEO of Competere and a former cleared advisor to the United States Trade Representative. Mr. Singham is a former advisor to the Secretary of State for International Trade of the UK. He is Chairman of the Growth Commission and Vice Chairman of the Trade Facilitation Commission. He has represented governments and multinational companies and has had a pivotal role in many major global economic shifts of the last 35 years including the transitions in the former Soviet Union, the opening of Latin America, the UK's exit from the EU and the global realignment resulting from the Trump imposition of unfair trade and reciprocal tariffs.

Routledge Focus on Economics and Finance

The fields of economics are constantly expanding and evolving. This growth presents challenges for readers trying to keep up with the latest important insights. Routledge Focus on Economics and Finance presents short books on the latest big topics, linking in with the most cutting-edge economics research.

Individually, each title in the series provides coverage of a key academic topic, whilst collectively the series forms a comprehensive collection across the whole spectrum of economics.

Capital Structure and Firm Performance
Global Financing Decisions among Listed Companies
Ewelina Sokołowska and Milad Zargartalebi

Health insurance in the United States of America
Austrian Perspectives on Interventionism before ObamaCare
Łukasz Jasiński

Financing for Development
Towards a New, Green Bretton Woods
Stefan Brunnhuber

Efficient Mutual Fund Markets
A Global Perspective
Stanisław Urbanski, Bartosz Rymkiewicz, Jacek Leśkow and Bartosz Stawiarski

International Trade, Regulation and the Global Economy
The Impact of Anti-Competitive Market Distortions
Shanker A. Singham

For more information about this series, please visit: www.routledge.com/Routledge-Focus-on-Economics-and-Finance/book-series/RFEF

International Trade, Regulation and the Global Economy

The Impact of Anti-Competitive Market Distortions

Shanker A. Singham

Routledge
Taylor & Francis Group
LONDON AND NEW YORK

First published 2026
by Routledge
4 Park Square, Milton Park, Abingdon, Oxon OX14 4RN

and by Routledge
605 Third Avenue, New York, NY 10158

Routledge is an imprint of the Taylor & Francis Group, an informa business

British Library Cataloguing-in-Publication Data
A catalogue record for this book is available from the British Library

ISBN: 978-1-032-94416-6 (hbk)
ISBN: 978-1-032-94417-3 (pbk)
ISBN: 978-1-003-57060-8 (ebk)

DOI: 10.4324/9781003570608

Typeset in Times New Roman
by Apex CoVantage, LLC

This book is dedicated to my wife, Mellicent, the sine qua non of my life in this world, and to my three children, Tanaquil, Tristan and Jacques.

This book is dedicated to my [illegible]

[illegible]

[illegible]

Contents

Figures and Tables

Chapter 1

Chapter 2

Chapter 3

Chapter 4

Chapter 5

Foreword

In the intricate realm of international trade, few challenges are as pervasive and detrimental as Anti-Competitive Market Distortions (ACMDs). These distortions, often stemming from government actions that favour certain private interests or blur the distinction between private and public, undermine the competitive process, stifle innovation and harm consumer welfare.

Twenty-five years ago, Shanker A. Singham coined the phrase anti-competitive market distortions (ACMDs) to describe barriers that got in the way of willing buyers and willing sellers meeting human needs in voluntary exchange. This could include trade barriers, anti-competitive regulations and other non-tariff barriers, and failure to protect property rights, especially intellectual property. As I recall, that was about the time we first met. Since then, he has been at the forefront of the development of the economic models to put metrics on the scale of these ACMDs.

I also recall "borrowing" his first book from an anti-trust colleague in New Zealand around that time (it remained on my shelf unreturned for many years). It is, therefore, a particular pleasure to have the opportunity to offer the preface to this one. This volume is now the fourth book which Shanker A. Singham has written on the subject of distortions and the link between what happens inside markets and their trade effects over almost 20 years. He has been one of the few voices insisting that this link exists and that our collective failure to deal with it has led to many of the economic problems we face today.

In this seminal work, Mr. Singham delves deep into the nature, origins and ramifications of ACMDs. He offers a comprehensive analysis of how these distortions manifest themselves across various markets and jurisdictions and lays out comprehensive economic models that can be used to measure distortions. Beyond identification, and quantification, complex as that exercise is, he also proposes actionable strategies for policymakers, businesses and international institutions to mitigate and ultimately eliminate the adverse effects of ACMDs.

It is vital therefore that we have reliable metrics to measure distortions so we can tell what the effect on our economies actually is. This is also very important in understanding the effects on trade of ACMDs.

As an old trade hand who has had to deal day to day with the consequences of ACMDs in trade policy and trade negotiations, I can attest to the critical importance of this work. Mr. Singham's insights provide not only a diagnostic tool but also a roadmap towards more equitable and efficient markets. His emphasis on the synergy between robust competition policies, transparent regulatory frameworks and the protection of property rights serves as a clarion call for nations aiming to foster sustainable economic growth.

In light of the Trump Administration's recent implementation of "reciprocal tariffs", designed to match the tariffs imposed by other countries on US exports, I suspect that the insights presented in this book will prove particularly timely and vital. These policy shifts underscore the necessity for a nuanced understanding of Anti-Competitive Market Distortions (ACMDs) and their global implications. Mr. Singham's comprehensive analysis offers invaluable guidance for policymakers, trade negotiators and business leaders navigating this evolving landscape, providing strategies to promote open competition and mitigate the adverse effects of distortionary measures. This book is an indispensable resource for anyone engaged in the fields of international trade, economics and public policy. It challenges us to rethink somewhat piecemeal and disconnected policy approaches in a more coherent way. But it has a practical purpose: to support and enhance collective effort towards dismantling the barriers that hinder true market competition and voluntary exchange. Through Mr. Singham's expertise and vision, we are equipped to confront the complexities of ACMDs and move towards a more open and prosperous global economy.

Crawford has a lengthy background in trade policy and trade negotiations both inside and outside national governments. This has included being the lead trade official for New Zealand (2008–11) and the United Kingdom (2017–24).

Sir Crawford Falconer

Acknowledgements

The economic models that I have developed over the last 20 years have involved many different teams, and I am deeply grateful for the hard work and commitment of all of them. Some people deserve special mention. Professor Srini Rangan, at Babson College, has been of immense value to all our different models and it is right that his name is on the original Singham–Rangan–Bradley model from which much of this work developed. I am also thankful to the Cebr team led by Douglas McWilliams that helped on refining and further simplifying the SRB model, as well as developing the Agency Based Model (with Cristian Niculescu-Marcu). I am also indebted to Christine McDaniel and Tom Stratmann at Mercatus and George Mason University, respectively, who have helped to refine this econometric tool and are a major reason for our confidence in the results. Finally, I am hugely thankful to David Silver, formerly head of Johns Hopkins Applied Physics lab, for being willing to engage with me on the pursuit of a probabilistic model drawn from the physical sciences. Our many afternoons developing this model is, I feel, only the start of a whole new approach to the problem of distortions which could properly integrate dynamic effects and more accurately explain the nature and intensity of voluntary exchanges between willing buyers and willing sellers.

1 The Implications of Recent Trade History

1.1 Introduction

Economic growth has contributed to significant economic gains for the world. These gains have been arguably greatest for developing countries with a billion people lifted out of absolute (less than $1 per day) poverty. In the period between 1947 and 2008, almost all the world's people were lifted out of absolute poverty. This is a remarkable achievement. Despite the achievement, the projected potential gains for global growth, which were anticipated in the mid-1990s, have not been realised. This is partly due to policy mistakes made by the developed world in the period between the mid-1990s and now and lack of action taken by the developed world to combat the impact of policies in other countries that tend to destroy global wealth. A major way in which global growth has been held back and how global wealth has been destroyed is through what we have termed anti-competitive market distortions (ACMDs). This chapter will examine the impact of these ACMDs on the global economy in the last 30 years and how their continued prevalence has damaged the global economy.

There are two distinct problems to solve. First, what role do market distortions play in damaging trade and competition in countries? This can be approximated using econometric modelling of the impact of distortions across the dimensions of trade, competition and property rights in a general sense. The second and related problem is how best countries whose producers do not benefit from ACMDs should deal with producers in countries that do in international trade. In the first case, a country is damaging its own GDP per capita by distorting its market in these ways. In the second case, countries are damaging their trading partners through the distortion in their markets. Both issues need to be addressed, but the tools to address them are slightly different.

The curve in Figure 1.1 illustrates the uniqueness of the period from 1947 to 2008. By 1947, though trade liberalisation gains had not been realised, a large percentage of GDP per capita had been realised, indicating a dramatic rise in the early 19th century itself to reflect the gains from the industrial revolution.

DOI: 10.4324/9781003570608-1

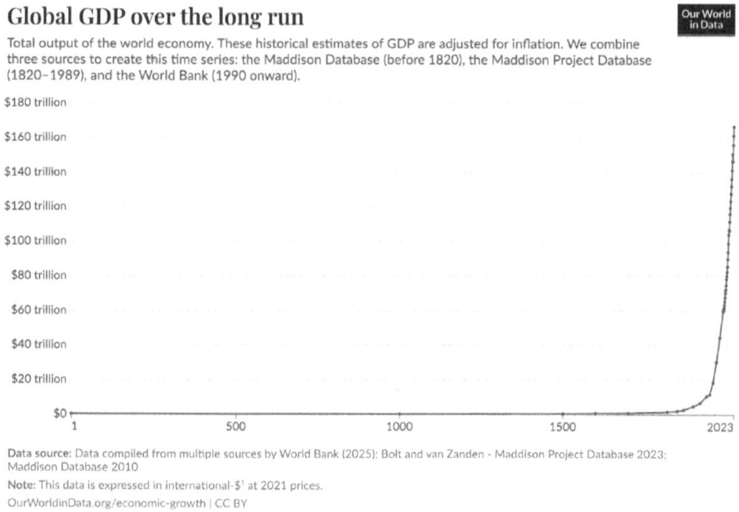

Figure 1.1 Reflections on the Power of the International Trading System to Lift People out of Poverty

The normal state of human beings is poverty and war. This has been the natural state for almost all human history with the 70-year or so post-war to the global financial crisis period, being a unique interregnum between thousands of years of poverty and conflict. There are many reasons for this, but certainly, the post-war international trading system and what it spawned in the global economy can take its share of the credit.

The General Agreement on Tariffs and Trade (GATT) system that followed the end of the Second World War systematically lowered the high tariffs that were applied to industrial goods. Initially, as countries came together to lower trade barriers on the basis that countries that trade together are less likely to go to war, their vision was much more comprehensive than just reducing trade tariffs on industrial goods. What was envisaged was an International Trade Organization (ITO) that would cover all the potential barriers to trade and agriculture and deal with other barriers such as anti-competitive business practices, cartels, monopolies and the like. The ITO even envisaged disciplines on labour and environmental rules, reaching well behind the border in several ways. Ironically, precisely because of this attempt to discipline what countries did in their own markets, the US Congress refused to allow this limitation on domestic authority and rejected the deal. What was left was a contract between GATT members to do the most basic of things – reduction on industrial goods tariffs. Even though this was a limited aspiration, its economic effect was enormous. Over the three decades between the 1940s and

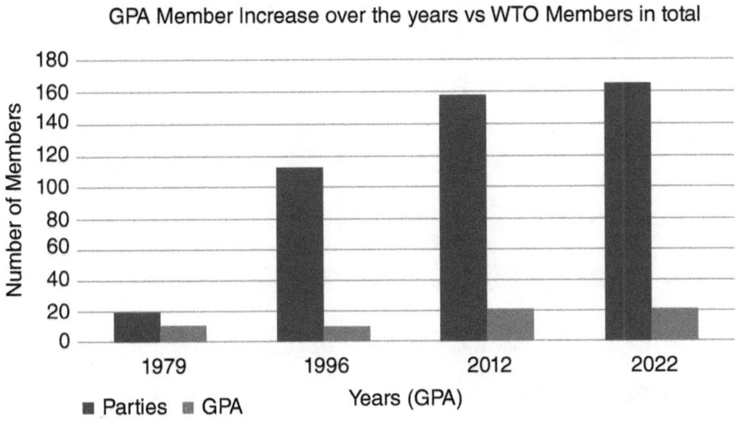

Figure 1.2 GPA New Member Increase over the Years (1979–2022)

1970s, industrial goods tariffs were slashed. This made it possible for companies to trade all over the world and develop complex supply chains where key inputs were produced in the most efficient manner possible. No longer was it necessary to build a factory in a country to reach its market. Inefficiencies were removed, and the transnational company flourished.

In the 1970s, it became obvious that many countries were free riding on the benefits of the tariff reductions in certain (primarily developed) countries. It was decided that if these countries wanted to go further in liberalisation and the free riders were not prepared to do so also, then they should be allowed to negotiate deeper liberalisation on a plurilateral basis (this occurred in the Tokyo Round for government procurement, for example). This meant that the benefits of those agreements would not be spread to all GATT members – a major departure from the multilateral principles. The theory was that if a small number of countries pushed liberalisation, the rest could be added, but this did not really occur in the case of the Government Procurement Agreement (GPA), where the addition of new members was a relatively slow process (See Figure 1.2 above).

On the other hand, the new plurilateral direction of the GATT did enable members to come together to do precisely what the developed country members wanted in the 1970s. In 1986, a much more comprehensive round was initiated (the Uruguay Round, launched in 1986 and concluded in 1994). This in part recognised the fact that many of these issues were impeding the gains from liberalisation being achieved and represented a partial return to the thinking, which led to the initial ITO in 1947, some 50 years later.

Growth rates dramatically increased in the decades after the GATT system was launched all the way through the 1980s and 1990s. However, growth

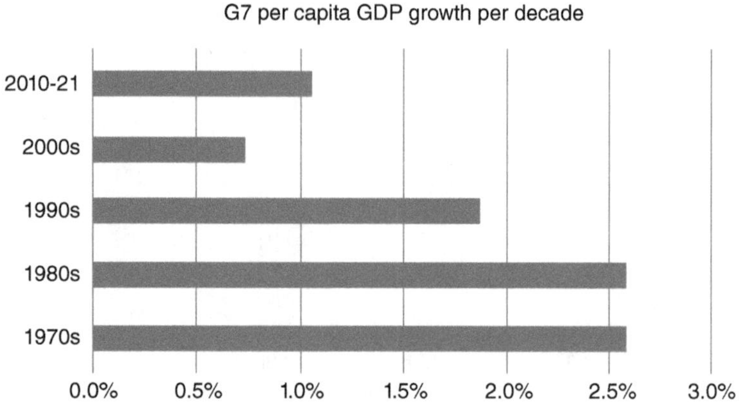

Figure 1.3 G7 Countries' Per Capita GDP Growth (1970–2021)

rates started to slow down counterintuitively from the 2000s to now (see Figure 1.3).

This is remarkable because of the events that occurred in the 1990s, which should have instead led to dramatically and rapidly increasing economic growth. First, there were significant new markets that entered the global system. India came out of import substitution in 1991, the Uruguay Round concluded in 1994 and China's WTO accession was complete in 2001. The former Soviet bloc emerged as part of the WTO system, and many joined the European Union after the fall of the Berlin Wall in 1989, and the apertura in Latin America occurred in 1992. By any judgement, all these events should have heralded a massive increase in global growth, but this did not happen.

The reduction in trade barriers also paved the way for a rapid rise in technological improvements, leading to a staggering increase in computing power. This should also have led to much greater efficiencies as the number of employees needed to generate $1 million of revenue plunged. But again, this powerful productivity-enhancing effect did not seem to find its way into the rate of increase of the GDP per capita numbers. In addition to increasing market distortions in the round, there was a rapid increase in the number of subsidies in the world since 2008.[1] The number of subsidies granted went from 48 in 2008 to over 5,000 in 2020.

This chapter contends that while there are, no doubt, many reasons for this, a significant driver lies in the policy choices made by G7 nations in the regulation of their own markets and the inability of the global system to deal with policy choices in some of these newer markets that had a damaging effect on global growth. This combination has led to the parlous situation, which the global economy faces now and has contributed to the extremely sluggish

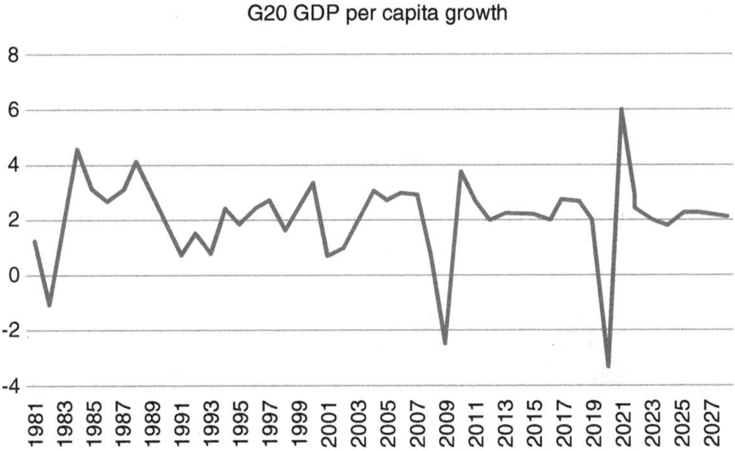

Figure 1.4 G20 Countries' Per Capita GDP Growth (1981–2023) with Forecast for 2024–2027

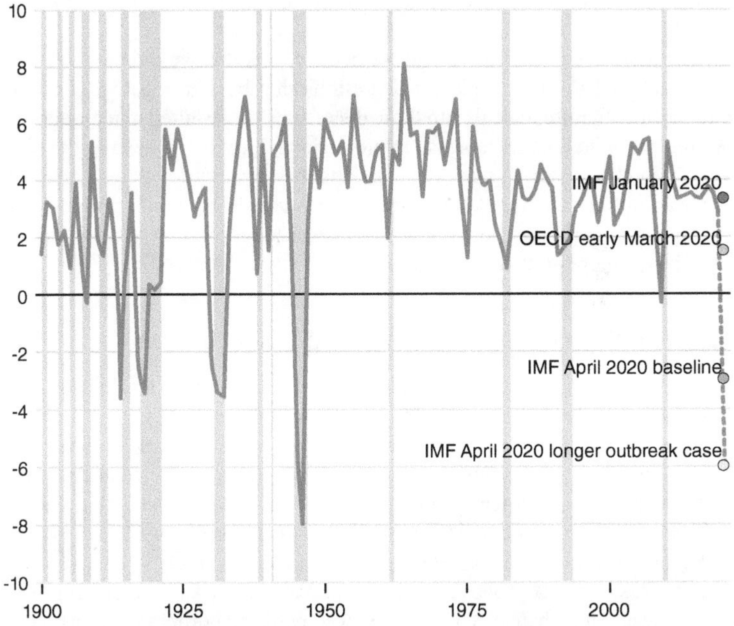

Figure 1.5 IEA-Based IMF World Economic Outlook (January and April 2020), OECD Interim Economic Outlook Forecasts (March 2020) and Maddison Project Database (2018).

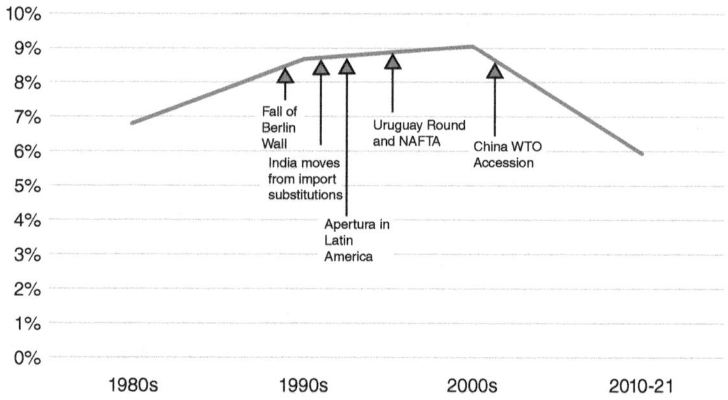

Figure 1.6 Events That Should Have Led to a Dramatic Increase in the Rate of Economic Growth

growth in the United States, Western Europe and Japan since the turn of the century (See Figures 1.4–1.6).

The root cause of this problem, we believe, was that we did not deal with or we allowed to expand market distortions that have a negative effect on competition. Failure to deal with these distortions has resulted in major political impacts – fuelling an increase in protectionism (which is seen as the only way to combat distortions in other markets that have trade effects), a rise in localisation rules and regulatory barriers. This creates a vicious circle of progressively less and less liberalisation, less and less economic growth, which only fosters more political responses.

1.2 The Nature of New International Trade Problems

There are two major problems in international trade, which are increasingly manifesting themselves and creating several frictions.

First, increasingly behind the border, barriers and market distortions (anti-competitive market distortions or ACMDs) have replaced tariffs as the preferred method of protection in many areas. In our view, the global trading system has not been able to deal with this reality appropriately.

Second, several issues outside the traditional trade remit have been brought into the trade agenda. These include issues like labour and the environment and, now, climate change. This has renewed calls for border tax adjustments or dual tariffs on an ex ante basis. This is in sharp tension with the World Trade Organization's (WTO's) long-standing principle of technological neutrality and focus on outcomes as opposed to discriminating on the basis of the way products are produced.

The problem is that it is too easy to hide protectionist impulses in concerns about the manner of production, and once a different tariff applies, it will be very difficult to remove. The result will be to significantly damage the liberalisation process itself, leading to severe harm to the global economy at a critical time as we recover from COVID-19.

Understanding what market distortions are will help us to better understand how they can be tackled, and how a systematic across-the-board reduction in ACMDs can lead to a much more rapid economic growth.

Note

1 OECD, Subsidies. (2022). *Competition and Trade, OECD Competition Policy Roundtable Background Note*, available here.

2 The Danger Anti-Competitive Market Distortions Present to the International Economic System

2.1 Introduction to ACMDs

Anti-Competitive Market Distortions, or ACMDs, refer to government-imposed restrictions on competition.

Three fundamental principles are critical to this work.

1. Wealth (by which we mean the realisation of ideas measured by money as a by-product) can be created or destroyed.
2. Wealth is easier to destroy than to create.
3. The most powerful force we know of to create wealth is competition.

Unpicking these, wealth creation means the successful realisation of ideas. These ideas become crystallised into things that can be bought and sold if the underlying forces at play in an economy allow them to be crystallised. Money is merely a measurement device, a way for us to determine how effective this wealth creation process is.

Our goal must be an economy where willing buyers and sellers come together to meet human needs in voluntary exchange without distortions that impede their ability to "exchange". In such a world, the distance between idea generation and idea crystallisation is as small as possible. The problem is that market distortions of one type or another get in the way of this process and therefore contribute to wealth destruction. Because wealth is easier to destroy than create, the "equilibrium" position for an economic system in a given country is actually one of maximal distortion, leading to poverty and war, not prosperity and peace. That is why I have written that it is poverty and war that have been the natural state of man throughout the last ten thousand years. The period of prosperity and peace between 1947 and 2006 is a highly unusual period in human history. We may never see it again. We will never see it again unless we work very hard to lift economic systems out of their natural, highly distorted equilibrium state.

I have written extensively about market distortions for over 20 years.[1] I have also dealt with the issue extensively in my 2007 book, *A General Theory of*

DOI: 10.4324/9781003570608-2

Trade and Competition: Trade Liberalisation and Competitive Markets (CMP (2007). Formally, Abbott and Singham[2] have defined ACMDs as those that "involve government actions that empower certain private interests to obtain or retain artificial competitive advantages over their rivals be they foreign or domestic".

I have also discussed market distortions in a working paper for the Council on Foreign Relations, Freeing the Global Market by Curbing Regulatory Distortions.[3] This paper included an inventory of distortions and explained why they have a pernicious impact on international trade.

Having identified that ACMDs present a pernicious problem in international trade, the lack of a quantum of the impact of these distortions made it very difficult to evaluate the scale of the problem. It was therefore necessary to research different ways of evaluating the harm posed by ACMDs. Singham and Rangan embarked on this exercise with a series of papers from 2014.[4] Singham and Rangan also published two papers introducing the economic analysis of ACMDs in 2016 for the Legatum Institute.[5] That work is the precursor to this book and the modifications and adaptations to the model used.

I and my co-authors have provided an inventory of the kinds of ACMDs that prevail around the world.[6] Broadly speaking, they consist of government practices of whatever kind that damage the ordinary process of market competition. Anything that interferes with voluntary exchanges between willing buyers and willing sellers can (not must) damage market competition. Many government distortions do not have effects on market competition, and we are not concerned with these. An attempt to remove ACMDs is not necessarily deregulation, but it is a move towards pro-competitive regulation. Deregulation and pro-competitive regulation are only the same if the regulatory system is anti-competitive to start with. ACMDs fall into several categories:

1) Those that limit the supply of goods, leading to price increases.
2) Those that prevent market contestability for exporters through regulatory barriers in the import market (such as distribution restraints that only apply to foreign suppliers).
3) Those that artificially lower costs for certain producers allowing them to outcompete producers subject to normal market forces.
4) Failure to protect property rights (including intellectual property rights) in ways that change the cost structure of certain market participants in ways that ordinary market forces operating in a property rights protecting environment would not allow.
5) Private anti-competitive practices that may be tolerated or encouraged by government regulation even as the private practices themselves are well known to antitrust law.
6) The actions of government agencies including competition agencies ostensibly to promote competition, but whose actions lead to damage to market competition.

ACMDs can be particularly harmful (as distinct from private anti-competitive behaviour), as they are imposed by the government. Therefore, they enjoy state-backed power and the force of law. Consequently, they may be impervious to attenuation by ordinary market processes. One specific example of an ACMD in the environmental area is as follows.

Consider a market, where firms generate a certain level of pollution. Suppose that the government orders all firms to cut down on pollution by the same amount. However, assume there is no cap-and-trade system in place, whereby firms with high costs of reducing pollution can buy permits from other firms at a price lower than its cost of reducing pollution. In such a case, a high-cost firm may have access to low-cost pollution reduction technology and a low-cost firm may be handicapped by not having such access. In that case, a low-cost firm may likely exit and the resulting reduction in the competition may be even more detrimental to consumer welfare. In this less competitive market, the welfare benefit from reduced pollution could be offset by the welfare cost of reduced competition. This distortion can be termed as an ACMD.

It is only by fully understanding the metrics of ACMDs that we can really evaluate their impact. ACMDs can damage international trade flows as well as distorting markets in ways that reduce competition and destroy wealth out of the economy. Hence, ACMDs are just as relevant to the international trade agenda as they are to the domestic regulatory agenda. Policymakers would greatly benefit from understanding the cost of ACMDs and how they relate to domestic regulatory promulgation. The OECD in its regulatory toolkit and competition assessment has advised policymakers to promulgate regulation in ways that are the least anti-competitive possible consistent with a publicly stated, legitimate regulatory goal. Many countries include this sort of competition assessment in the ways they promulgate regulations, including considering the views of competition agencies. However, absent a robust metric to measure distortion, it is difficult for governments to properly evaluate the harm caused by certain types of regulation, and it is also impossible for the public to fully understand the impact of regulation so that they can properly weigh the costs and benefits of regulation and determine if the harm is justified by the importance of the regulatory objectives.

Economists have long recognised the prevalence and pernicious consequences of ACMDs. The complexity and breadth of this issue, however, have made it an especially difficult one for policymakers to tackle. In this book, we attempt to break down the impact of ACMDs on productivity. We then attempt to examine the impact of reducing ACMDs in the United Kingdom, by trying to predict the impact on GDP per capita, over a 15-year period.

If we can develop metrics to measure ACMDs, there are a number of policy consequences that are of great value. These include allowing governments to tariffficate market distortions in the markets of trading partners, which allows a nuanced approach to issues like the US–China trade dispute (as opposed to the imposition of a tariff regardless of evidence of ACMDs in China). Such a policy would have the advantage of incentivising the party, which has the ACMDs to actually lower them (and thereby benefit from the lower tariff), as well as enabling countries to signal to their trading partners that they are open to imports, which are efficiently produced because of the consumer welfare gains for their economies.

Policymakers can also improve the quality of their own regulatory promulgation processes. Under the OECD Regulatory Toolkit and Competition Assessment, governments should regulate in ways that are the least damaging to competition, consistent with a publicly stated, legitimate regulatory goal. If policymakers had a sense of the effect of ACMDs in their own markets on their own economic output, this would be tremendously valuable in coming to better regulatory decisions. It would also be invaluable in ensuring that legislators can properly evaluate the regulatory goal and the cost of the ACMD and make informed decisions.

Such a metric would also inform the public debate and ensure that this is actually being carried out in a manner that balances the regulatory objectives that need to be properly and clearly stated, and the cost of the ACMDs to the economy. Too often in public debate, a knee jerk response to a perceived market failure occurs without any attempt to present, much less understand the economic evidence.

A metric will also tell us something about the scale of the economic impact of ACMDs. In the past, it has been assumed that reduction of trade barriers is where the largest economic gains are to be found, and reduction of distortions is important but not of the same order of magnitude. A metric will enable us to evaluate this impact. A sense of the scale of this impact was developed in preliminary fashion by Cebr in 2019.[7] According to the Cebr report, imposing a distortion inside the border as opposed to at the border in an agency-based model led to a 37 per cent reduction in output versus an 11 per cent reduction of output for an equivalent border measure. This suggests that the impact of ACMDs might be much higher than previously supposed.

There are several ways of tackling the problem. We have developed both an econometric and an agency-based model for getting a sense of the quantum.

There are three major impacts of ACMDs in global markets, which need to be addressed differently.

1. ACMDs distort the domestic market. This purely domestic impact can be measured using a range of models we describe later.
2. ACMDs artificially lower costs of exporters and so damage import markets. A different set of metrics need to be used here to support defensive trade tools and mechanisms.
3. ACMDs can be used as barriers to import, in effect negating market access concessions in trade agreements by making markets effectively uncontestable.

In all three cases, ACMDs have a negative impact on global welfare, which is why it is important that mechanisms can be found to deal with them. We will first look at ACMD distortion of domestic (and in the case of the agency-based model, the global market) and then look at impacts on trade.

2.2 An Agency-Based Model to Understand ACMDs

Working with partners in the Centre for Economics and Business Research (Cebr), we have established an agency-based model.[8]

Noted in the Cebr study:

> The model suggests that between- and within-country trade distortions have a substantial effect on country and global levels of output. For example, a between-country trade distortion of 25% acts to lower global output relative to the benchmark case with no distortions by around 4%. A within-country trade distortion of 25% acts to lower global output relative to the benchmark case with no distortions by around 14%. When both types of distortion are present, output is approximately 17% lower than the benchmark case with no distortions. While further investigation is required, the joint effect of the two types of distortions would appear to be "broadly" linear (i.e. the sum of the two partial effects of each distortion).

Figure 7 of the Cebr study expresses the global output that arises with between-country trade distortions as a percentage of global output in the benchmark case. We see global output (averaged over time) is falling with the degree of between-country trade distortion. Output is 4 per cent lower when 25 per cent of consumers are unable to access foreign markets; 7 per cent lower when half of consumers are unable to access foreign markets; and 10 per cent lower when 75 per cent of consumers are unable to access foreign markets. Note that these percentage falls in output also hold for changes in output in both country A and country B, respectively. This is unsurprising given that the distribution of consumers and firms is assumed to be identical in both countries. As stated, our focus is with the effects on global output, rather than any distributional implications across countries. We also see the impact on costs of distortions. Figure 8 expresses the unconditional average cost that arises with distortions as a percentage of the unconditional average cost with no distortions (the benchmark case). Average cost is 11 per cent higher when 25 per cent of consumers are unable to access foreign markets; 17 per cent higher when half of consumers are unable to access foreign markets; 24 per cent higher when 75 per cent of consumers are unable to access foreign markets; and finally, 29 per cent higher when consumer-firm trade is entirely "autarkic".

Figure 9 of the Cebr study expresses the global output that arises with within-country trade distortions as a percentage of global output in the benchmark case. Unsurprisingly, global output is falling with these distortions because they prevent mutually beneficial trades from taking place. Output is 12 per cent lower when approximately 25 per cent of transactions between consumers and firms that would otherwise go ahead do not due to distortions. Output largely falls linearly with the distortion, ultimately falling to zero (an extreme case) when no transactions can take place.

However, what is clear is that the impact of in-country distortions on global output is around three times more significant than the same type of distortion applied at the border.

2.3 Analysing Other Studies

There have been a number of other studies that have sought to measure the impact on GDP or GDP per capita of anti-competitive regulation. In Australia, the impact of the national competition policy that included tariff reform as well as regulatory reform can be seen below.

Exhibit 6 from ACCC Study: Forecast growth and revenue benefits from NCP change (See Figure 2.1 below).

An ex post analysis from the Australian productivity commission had also suggested that a 2.5 per cent gain in GDP had been achieved but this was spread over a much smaller group of sectors and therefore likely considerably underestimated the actual dynamic efficiency gains.[9] The sectors included were urban water, gas, electricity, telecommunications, urban transport, ports and rail freight sectors.[10] The Australian study also considered distributional effects and found that the economic gains were well spread out across all income brackets. The study also connected the improvement in trade openness with the improvement in competition in key sectors achieved not only

Item	*Description*
Growth	
Real GDP	5.5%
Real consumption	$9 billion pa
Real wages	3% increase
Employment	30,000 more jobs
Revenue	
Commonwealth	$5.9 billion
States, Territories, local government	$3.0 billion

Figure 2.1 ACCC Study: Forecast Growth and Revenue Benefits from National Competition Policy

through private competition law implementation but also by a pro-competitive approach to regulation – in other words, a reduction in ACMDs.

A recent study by Singla of the University of Goethe reveals that 31–37 per cent of market share gain for incumbents is attributable to the US federal regulation.[11] In other words, incumbents lobby for anti-competitive regulation to exclude rivals very successfully. A study of European regulation by ECIPE suggest that 3–4 per cent of GDP gains are possible by reducing ACMDs.[12]

The Growth Commission, in its papers 2 and 3, have identified a range of different studies that examine the impact on GDP per capita of anti-competitive regulation.[13] Increasingly, many researchers are finding that these impacts are significant – ranging between 3 per cent and 7 per cent of GDP per capita losses due to ACMDs. These metrics put the notion that ACMDs are primarily a developing world problem completely out of court. They also highlight the importance for policymakers to address them seriously.

The essence of ACMD theory is that it encompasses conventional trade theory, domestic distortions, property rights theory, and competition policy and industrial organisation theory into a single coherent and mutually reinforcing whole.

Notes

1 See, for example, Singham, Shanker A. (1999). Market Access and Market Contestability: Is the Difference Purely Semantics: A Business Perspective. *Brook. Journal of International Law* 25, 337; Singham, Shanker A. (2001, Summer). Advancing the Competition and Trade Policy Agenda: Public Sector Restraints on Trade in the Free Trade Area of the Americas. *International Antitrust Bulletin.*

Singham, Shanker A., and Sokol, D. Daniel. (2004). Public Sector Restraints; Behind the Border Trade Barriers. *Texas International Law Journal* 39, 625.

2 Abbott, Alden F., and Singham, Shanker. (2011, November). Enhancing Welfare by Attacking Anticompetitive Market Distortions. *Revue Concurrences* 4, 39547.

3 See Singham, Shanker. (2012, October). Freeing the Global Market: How to Boost the Economy by Curbing Regulatory Distortions. *Council for Foreign Relations*, available at https://www.cfr.org/sites/default/files/pdf/2012/09/CFR_WorkingPaper15_Singham.pdf

4 See Singham, Shanker A., and Rangan, U. Srinivasa. (2014, December). *The Effect of Anticompetitive Market Distortions (ACMDs) on Global Markets Concurrences.*

5 See Anti-Competitive Market Distortions and their Impact; A case study of India, Singham, Rangan, Bradley and Kiniry (https://img1.wsimg.com/blobby/go/bf4d316c-4c0b-4e87-8edb-350f819ee031/downloads/1cstfqts9_122710.pdf?ver=1603533215968); See also An Introduction to Anti-Competitive Market Distortions, Legatum Institute, September, 2016, available at https://img1.wsimg.com/blobby/

go/bf4d316c-4c0b-4e87-8edb-350f819ee031/downloads/1cste45av_640953.pdf?ver=1603533215968
6 See especially FN 3, 4 and 5.
7 See An Agent Based model of Trade; Market Distortions and Output, Cebr, 2019, February, available at: https://img1.wsimg.com/blobby/go/bf4d316c-4c0b-4e87–8edb-350f819ee031/downloads/Cebr%20Market%20Distortions%20Trade%20Report.pdf?ver=1603533215968.
8 Cebr. (2019, October). *An Agent-based Model of Trade: Market Distortions and Output*, available at https://img1.wsimg.com/blobby/go/bf4d316c-4c0b-4e87-8edb-350f819ee031/downloads/Cebr Market Distortions Trade Report.pdf
9 Address by Mr. Rod Sims, Making markets work for increased productivity and growth: the Australian experience address, available at https://www.accc.gov.au/about-us/media/speeches/making-markets-work-for-increased-productivity-and-growth-the-australian-experience-address#ftn8
10 Australian Government Productivity Commission. (2005, February 28). *Review of National Competition Policy Reforms: Productivity Commission Inquiry Report*, available at https://www.pc.gov.au/inquiries/completed/national-competition-policy/report/ncp.pdf
11 Singla, Shikar. (2023, February 23). *Regulatory Costs and Market Power*. LawFin Working Paper No. 47.
12 Erixon, Frederik, Guinea, Oscar, and du Roy, Oscar. (2023, July). *If the EU was a State in the United States: Comparing Economic Growth between EU and US States*. ECIPE, available at https://ecipe.org/publications/comparing-economic-growth-between-eu-and-us-states/
13 See papers available at: Research – Page 2 – The Growth Commission.

3 The Application of a Number of Classical Economic Models to understand the Quantum of Distortion

3.1 Introduction to Econometric and Other Models

We have developed an econometric model to analyse distortions.[1] The model that we have developed is based on the notion that the three pillars of economic development are property rights protection, domestic competition and international competition.[2] Broadly, anti-competitive government policy affects the way the market functions through one of these three pillars.

3.1.1 Property Rights

The foundation of a productive economy is property rights protection. If property rights are left unprotected, the incentive to invest, compete and innovate is lost. If the returns from effort cannot be captured, can be taken away or cannot be regained if wrongly taken away, what incentive is there to exert effort? Furubotn and Pejovich[3] describe the nature of property rights in this way: "property rights do not refer to relations between men and things but, rather, to the sanctioned behavioral relations among men that arise from the existence of things and pertain to their use. . . . The prevailing system of property rights in the community, then, can be described as the set of economic and social relations defining the position of each individual with respect to the utilization of scarce resources" (p. 1139). The authors add in a footnote that "Roman Law, Common Law, Marx and Engels, and current legal and economic studies basically agree on this definition of property rights". In other words, the very nature of an economic transaction is defined by the right to property and this definition is not disputed. Property rights allow four things to occur: (1) investment to create the property (as in the case of intellectual property or IP and machinery); (2) investment to make the property more productive (as in the case of land, machinery and IP); (3) exploitation to get the maximum productivity out of it (as in the case of land, machinery, IP, etc.); and (4) transfer of property to another who might be able to do a better job of the first three instead of the current owner of the property (as in the case of land,

DOI: 10.4324/9781003570608-3

machinery and IP). All these lead to increased productivity, higher incomes and, thus, wealth and prosperity. So, a lack of property rights protection effectively undermines the ability of economic agents to operate effectively. It also undermines the process of competition, because property rights are what firms compete with. In developing countries in particular, establishing and enforcing property rights play a significant role in creating the preconditions for growth[4] [5] Therefore, all other factors influencing economic outcomes depend on the level and quality of property rights protection. We account for the fact that the effect of domestic competition and international competition on other factors depends on the level of property rights in our model and will discuss how we capture this in the next section.

The property rights protection indicator is constructed as follows. Intellectual property rights are themselves a type of property rights and are a crucial aspect of economic development.[6] Including this measure as a part of a property rights protection indicator was obvious and necessary. The other six subcategories are each different ways in which policy can ensure that the effort of agents cannot be wrongfully expropriated, that when a person's rights are violated, the process for righting that wrong is not prohibitively expensive,[7] and that the legal system itself has integrity. The subcategories of the property rights protection indicator follow the Heritage Foundation Index of Economic Freedom's criteria for grading countries in terms of property rights protection.[8]

3.1.2 Domestic Competition

Domestic competition plays a significant role in the efficiency of both domestic and foreign firms. Competition among firms encourages innovation and upgrading of production processes, as well as positive externalities in local markets.[9] Each of these features of competition has a positive impact on welfare, which justifies its inclusion as part of this index.

Typically, the term "competition policy" refers to regulations – and the enforcement of regulations – concerning restraint on competition created by private parties. Our domestic competition indicator is, instead, meant to capture the extent to which government policy itself restricts competitive behaviour.[10] Timothy Muris[11] highlights the importance of understanding and correcting restrictive government actions – not just private restrictions. He compares these two sources of competitive restrictions to the forks in a stream and states that "[p]rotecting competition by focusing solely on private restraints is like trying to stop the water flow . . . by blocking only one channel". Muris goes on to say that creating a system, which prevents anti-competitive behaviour by firms, but allows a government to dictate the same anticompetitive outcome that would have resulted from private action, has not eliminated the problem. "It has simply dictated the form that the problem will take".

Domestic competition here refers to the domestic policies affecting the way in which firms make decisions and interact with one another. Any policy that limits profit-maximising firms' ability to make their own decisions will reduce the score for domestic competition for a country.[12] If a policy reduces the ability of some subset of firms to make their own decisions while not restricting others in the same way, then the domestic policy score will be reduced. However, this does not mean that a country with no regulations controlling the decisions of firms will receive the highest score. The goal of this index and the scores it generates is to allow comparisons between countries regarding the degree to which policy is welfare-maximising. If welfare is to be maximised, then some government regulation may be appropriate in many contexts. For example, if a market can be characterised as a natural monopoly, appropriately tailored government regulation may be crucial for welfare maximisation.[13] If there are true market failures that are not being handled adequately through purely private action (severe adverse health effects from pollution, a shortage of funds for post-secondary education, harmfully discriminatory practices, etc.), then government regulation may be necessary.[14] These antitrust or industrial organisation types of regulations are part of the domestic competition score. No judgement is made as far as the exact specification of the regulation. Instead, the effectiveness of antitrust policy and the cost of adhering to different policies are the measures used.

The domestic competition score is higher when firms are able to make their own decisions because we are trying to evaluate how well domestic policies promote competitive behaviour. It is constructed as follows. Competitive behaviour refers to the behaviour firms exhibit in a particular market, which will maximise welfare within the market. Therefore, the domestic competition score is higher when policies respond to market failures and antitrust violations efficiently, but otherwise do not interfere with or dictate firm behaviour. This is because the behaviour of profit maximising firms – faced with demand from the market, the decisions of competitors, no market failures and no antitrust violations – will produce and charge a price that generates the welfare-maximising equilibrium. That is, once any market failures are corrected for, firms will behave in a way which maximises welfare. Of course, in practice, it is often very difficult or impossible to fully correct a market failure. However, some countries will do a better job than others in choosing and implementing policies that effectively respond to market failures. The closer a country is to actually eliminating a market failure, the closer it will be to moving a market towards its welfare-maximising equilibrium.[15]

The domestic competition indicator is defined by infrastructure[16] and the policies concerning how firms make decisions. Infrastructure and the efficiency with which it is built have serious implications for the competitiveness of a country. Reliable, well-maintained infrastructure is a crucial component of efficient markets. Here, infrastructure reflects each type of infrastructure in an economy. Labour regulations are defined by how free firms are to hire and fire employees, as well as how firms are then allowed to utilise those workers. Restrictions on the hiring and firing process or deployment of labour decisions will reduce the score for domestic competition. The less flexible policy makes the labour force, the higher the cost of production will be because firms will have to work around or suffer the restriction of each policy. Regulatory promulgation process refers to how laws are created. If the government is allowed to make decisions based on favouritism and the process is not transparent, anti-competitive market distortions (ACMDs) can be created at will. There will be no need to disguise them as market failures, or if they are disguised, they will be very difficult to recognise. Industrial organisation policies refer to the regulations to which firms must adhere to participate in a market and how antitrust deals with anticompetitive behaviour when it arises. All these areas impact a firm's ability to make their own profit-maximising decisions.

3.1.3 International Competition

International competition refers to the degree to which a country allows foreign firms to access its domestic market and the degree to which it allows domestic firms to access foreign markets. Any restriction on the free flow of trade which is not the correction to a market failure will reduce the score for international competition. Greater access to a wider variety of goods benefits consumers and greater access to less expensive or higher quality inputs benefits firms. Also, exposing firms to potentially more efficient foreign firms promotes innovation. All these forces combine to generate gains in welfare.[17]

International competition refers to how open a country is to interacting with foreign markets (a measure of the openness of its trade policy). The policies which reduce the score here are those that make it more costly or burdensome to transact internationally. The indicator is constructed as follows. Tariffs and procedural burden directly affect the flow of goods. Financial restrictions affect the flow of capital. The freedom of foreigners to visit is a measure reflecting the general openness of the economy to outsiders visiting. A policy that restricts visitation by foreigners would make it more difficult for foreign firms to have a presence in an economy. If any of these categories is restrictive, it will be more difficult for trade to occur. The Washington Consensus[18] also noted the importance of eliminating distortionary trade policies applied differently in different areas.[19] Import liberalisation is seen as particularly important because it eliminates the export disadvantage created by restricted access to less expensive imported intermediate goods. This type of ACMD is exactly what we are trying to capture with our international competition index.

3.1.4 Combined Effects

An important point to be made is that if one of these three areas is improved while the other two are left in a poor condition, the impact on productivity will be reduced or reversed. For example, if domestic competition is improved by making it faster and less costly for domestic firms to start a business but property rights are left unprotected and international competition is prevented, the impact on productivity will likely be zero because firms will still be uncertain about entering the market (because their property can be expropriated, e.g.) and will not need to compete as fiercely as they would in the face of foreign competition.

Each of the three categories has an impact on how an improvement in the other categories will be realised in terms of productivity. As stated previously, without property rights protection, agents cannot act in their own economic interests. This means that without property rights protection, improvements in the other two categories will have no effect on the determinants of productivity. Domestic competition determines the structure of a domestic market, which determines the equilibrium of each domestic market. If firms are not allowed to decide how they will behave, then imported foreign goods will enter an inefficient market and face inefficient constraints on their position in that market. It is possible that distorted domestic competition may help or hurt foreign firms. Similarly, international competition policies can prevent foreign firms from entering the domestic market or may prevent domestic firms from reaching foreign markets. In either case, the total effect in the long run will be a reduction of welfare.[20] Also, improving each of these three areas simultaneously will have a combined effect. If a country can correct the ACMDs in every area, it can move towards its optimal welfare level. Leaving ACMDs uncorrected in any area will negatively affect the benefits from correcting other ACMDs.

3.2 The Model

We model productivity as a function of factors, which have a direct impact on productivity in a country. These factors are themselves influenced by the policy decisions of a country. The factors affecting productivity are stock of foreign direct investment, stock of capital provided by the financial sector, health expenditures, educational attainment, fuel exports and ore and metal exports. The policy decisions are captured using our three indicators: property rights protection, domestic competition, and international competition. The structure of the estimation and the results are described below.

Productivity is measured in terms of GDP per capita. We estimate a reduced-form model to determine the factors that affect productivity. These factors are themselves influenced by the scores for domestic competition, international competition, and property rights protection. Our productivity model is:

$$\log \textit{of GDP per cap} = \beta_0 + \beta_1 * \log \textit{of FDI stock} + \beta_2 * \textit{Health Expenditures per cap} + \beta_3 * \textit{Domestic credit stock} + \beta_4 * \textit{School persistence} + \beta_5 * \textit{Fuel exports} + \beta_6 * \textit{Ore and Metal exports}$$

The *log of FDI stock* variable is the logarithm of the stock of Foreign Direct Investment per capita in a given country in a given year[21] and represents the stock of foreign capital available to each person in a given country in a given year. The *Health expenditures per cap* variable is a dollar value per person spent on health care in a country in a given year and it captures the influence of overall health in a country. *Domestic credit stock* is measured as the value of credit provided in an economy by its own financial sector and is reported as a percentage of GDP. This captures the available credit in an economy from its own financial sector. *School persistence* measures the portion of the population that reports to have completed primary school and/or advanced to secondary school. This controls for the human capital stock within a country. *Fuel exports* and *Ore and Metal exports*[22] are both reported as percentages of total merchandise exports and are both controls for differences in productivity, which arise from the existence of natural resources within a country.

The specification of this productivity function follows theoretically from Robert Solow's critique of productivity growth regressions.[23] Solow argues for the use of productivity as the left-hand side variable and using factors directly influencing productivity on the right-hand side. Our desire to find the impact of policies on productivity also led to the decision to specify our regression using productivity as the dependent variable because it is differences in productivity – not growth – that we are trying to capture. We want to know how ACMDs are impeding economic efficiency and, thus, we want to know what level of productivity countries could reach absent all ACMDs. The path to that particular level of productivity is important and interesting, but it is a separate issue from the one we are exploring here.

Our right-hand side variables also extend from the Solow critique. The types of variables recommended to be used on the right-hand side can be classified into four categories: economic factors, institutions, social base and physical base.[24] These categories are partially captured by the variables in our productivity function but are also covered through our ACMD category scores. For further inspiration for specifying our productivity function, we returned also to the traditional Solow model of productivity, which models productivity as a function of capital and labour.[25],[26] In addition to the traditional approach, our model fully subscribes to the notion of the importance of total factor productivity. We will now discuss the factors directly affecting productivity and how the property rights protection, domestic competition, and international competition scores influence these factors.

3.2.1 Domestic Stock Credit

In our model, the effect of capital on productivity includes financial capital and natural resources. *Domestic credit stock* is a measure of the capital provided to the private sector from domestic financial institutions expressed as a percentage of GDP. The more credit available (the greater the supply), the easier it will be for firms and individuals to access that capital and then use it for productive activities. Because it is measured as a percent of GDP, the ease of access is relative to the size of the economy and, so, it is capturing the availability of credit given the size of the economy. This means that comparisons made across countries are picking up the relative ease of access to capital. Also, domestic credit available falls into the Solow critique category of "economic factors".

The amount of credit available domestically will depend on how well property rights are protected in a country. For example, the weaker the property rights, the less certainty borrowers and lenders have that the arrangement they agree upon will be the reality once the loan is disbursed. This will make lenders less willing to make funds available because the uncertainty generated by poor property rights protection means there is greater risk in lending. In general, the less certain property rights are, the less total investment there will be in an economy and the slower will be economic growth.[27]

All else equal, liberalising financial markets – and markets in general – will increase the supply of domestic credit, which leads to economic growth.[28] Improving the domestic competition score in a country can be thought of as liberalisation (with an emphasis on liberalisation in every sector and the added component of government transparency and accountability). However, the financial crises associated with liberalising financial markets in the 1990s provide an excellent example of why improving domestic competition alone will not create a thriving financial sector. Countries which liberalised their financial sectors in the 1990s failed to make necessary reforms in property rights protection, in international competition policies, and in other domestic competition areas. Examples of existing issues which became detrimental once financial markets were deregulated include the following: unsustainable fiscal policy, defence of unsustainable exchange rate pegs, absence of meaningful oversight and growing concern over deposit guarantees.[29]

Financial institutions are tied – either directly or indirectly through other institutions – to foreign capital. If access to foreign capital markets is restricted, then domestic credit will see a reduced supply in comparison to open access. It has been shown that when a country's access to foreign capital markets is restricted, it reduces the supply of domestic credit.[30] Therefore, policies which lower the international competition score of a country will lead to a tightening of domestic credit.

3.2.2 Stock of FDI

Another measure of capital is *log of FDI stock*. This measure captures the amount of foreign money that has come into a country and how that money is spread across the population on average. The stock of FDI is used instead of the change in FDI because the stock essentially tells us the amount of foreign money available to the average individual. Current flows, on the other hand, will slow down once the stock reaches a certain threshold and pick up if the stock starts to dwindle. The stock of FDI also reflects the openness of an economy. If trade is truly allowed to flow freely in and out of a country, then the FDI stock will be higher because the costs associated with investing will be reduced. FDI brings the, "needed capital, skills, and know-how, either producing goods needed for the domestic market or contributing new exports".[31] Thus, FDI falls into the Solow critique category of "economic factors".

Property rights play a significant role in the inflow of FDI. The positive relationship between property rights and FDI is due in large part to the roles played by intellectual property rights protection and protection from expropriation. The strength of intellectual property rights protection has a positive effect on FDI inflows[32] since greater intellectual property rights protection attracts investment in innovative technology.[33] Ensuring that property will not be expropriated is a necessary insurance for foreign entities considering investing in a country.[34] One of the reasons FDI is so low in developing countries when the potential returns are so high is what Lucas[35] called "political risk". Lucas described "political risk" as an imperfection or absence in the mechanism for enforcing international borrowing agreements. Put differently, one explanation for the reason FDI does not flow into developing countries where returns are greatest is because this relationship is a possible equilibrium when property rights are not protected.

Domestic competition-related policies also play an important role in attracting FDI. In particular, the less costly it is to start a business, the greater FDI inflows – especially in developing countries.[36] Improving domestic competition regulations can even make countries less abundant in natural resources more competitive in attracting FDI.[37] Even if trade is open between two countries and FDI is technically allowed to flow freely between them, a distorted domestic market creates uncertainty for foreign firms and reduces the likelihood of investing. The exception to this pattern would, of course, be a case where the foreign firm has political connections in the domestic market, which allow it to bypass the burdensome regulations.[38]

All else equal, reducing or removing trade barriers will increase FDI as firms considering investing into a particular country will now observe fewer barriers to investment. The degree to which open trade policies or free trade agreements positively influence FDI is entirely dependent on the "investment climate" and "political stability" in the host country.[39] Put differently, the quality of domestic competition and property rights protection in a country each combines with the quality of international competition policy to determine the amount of FDI entering the country. If any of these factors is poor, it will divert FDI to a more open, stable environment.[40]

3.2.3 Health Expenditures

The *Health expenditures per capita* variable is a proxy for health outcomes.[41] The initial goal was to measure health outcomes here, but an ideal single measure of health outcomes is difficult to define because there are many indications of overall health (life expectancy, infant mortality, malnutrition, etc.) and the data for each are not uniformly available. Health expenditures per person are a labour input in the original Solow context. All else equal, a healthier population will be more productive. Also, *Health expenditures per capita* falls into the "economic factors" and "social base" categories in the Solow critique context.

Property rights have a mixed effect on health expenditure. On the one hand, if property rights are protected, the returns to innovation can be captured by the innovator, which increases the incentive for people to enter the field and for the government to spend money in the health sector. On the other hand, health care is an industry that can generally be characterised by highly inelastic demand and the necessity of large financial and time investments for innovation. High costs and inelastic demand can lead to high prices for medications, equipment and training. In the face of such high costs, limited government resources may be diverted.[42] However, increased protection of property rights (particularly patent protection) has a positive impact on the availability of medications across countries.[43] So, property rights protection has an ambiguous effect on health expenditures on its own.

The negative effect on health expenditures from increased property rights protection is due primarily to increased prices. The sources of relatively high prices include inelastic demand, government price controls and other disincentives to enter a market (fixed costs of launching, potential competition from generics, etc.).[44] However, these issues apply to developing countries. As countries develop and property rights are more strongly protected, innovation becomes more common domestically (as highlighted earlier). Thus, strong property rights increase health expenditures when domestic competition and open trade are promoted because countries with these characteristics are stronger economically.

Domestic competition improvements will increase the quality of health services and, therefore, the return to health expenditures. One avenue through which this effect occurs is the potential for competition over patients and health insurance subscribers. If hospitals must compete for patients and insurers must compete for clients, quality will improve relative to the case where these entities are not allowed to compete. This is true even when price is regulated; though, a higher regulated price can also lead to higher quality of services. Furthermore, when prices are determined competitively, pries may not rise compared to the regulated price. It stands to reason that competition over insurers will lead hospitals to charge lower prices – particularly if insurers are competing over clients.[45]

Also, health expenditures have become linked to international trade relationships. Health services trade is a growing segment and the potential gains in health outcomes and, therefore, returns to health expenditures from trading health services openly have been documented.[46] These potential gains can make an important difference globally, as the demand for health services is predicted to grow as populations become "older, wealthier, and subject to more chronic disease".[47]

3.2.4 Fuel Exports and Ore and Metal Exports

The effect of natural resources on productivity is captured using *Fuel exports* and *Ore and Metal exports*. These factors clearly have a direct effect on our measure of productivity because GDP includes exports. When a large percent of manufacturing exports consists of these goods, the relative productivity of workers will be impacted. *Fuel exports* bias GDP per capita upwards because large export values can be generated with relatively few workers. Oil's share of GDP reaches almost as high as 50 per cent for some countries[48] and oil exports can reach a value equal to over 40 per cent of GDP.[49] *Ore and Metal exports* bias GDP per capita downwards because fairly low export values for the volume of goods produced are generated with relatively many workers.[50] Also, the types of infrastructure and other businesses that exist in high fuel-exporting and high ore and mineral-exporting countries are different from those that exist in other countries. So, these variables capture their direct effect on productivity as well as the indirect effect generated by the relative dependence of countries on these goods. Also, *Fuel exports* and *Ore and Metal exports* fall into the categories of "economic factors" and "physical base".

3.2.5 School Persistence

Finally, *School persistence* is our measure of human capital in a country. The more people who have reported to have completed primary school or attended some amount of secondary school, the better educated the population is. The higher the level of education, the more skilled the population and, therefore, the more productive the population.[51] Also, *School persistence* falls into the "economic factors" and "social base" categories in the Solow critique context.

3.2.6 Results

The coefficients in the productivity function are estimated using an ordinary least squares regression with heteroscedasticity robust standard errors. The results of this regression are given in Table 3.1 that follows.

Each variable is statistically significant at the 99 per cent confidence level and the regression as a whole explains about 90 per cent of the variance in GDP per capita between countries. This production function captures the determinants of productivity within a country at a given time with a high degree of accuracy. The mean absolute prediction error is about 4 per cent, which means that the above regression is roughly 96 per cent accurate when estimating GDP per capita when given the values for the independent variables.

Next, we evaluate the effect of improving a country's score in domestic competition, international competition and/or property rights protection on the stock of FDI, the stock of domestic credit and overall health in an economy. Our model counterintuitively shows that school persistence is largely uncorrelated with our policy indicators. This is likely because school

Table 3.1 Regression Results

	log of GDP per capita
log of FDI stock	0.362***
	(0.0254)
health expenditure	0.000258***
	(0.0000)
domestic credit provided by financial sector	0.00197***
	(0.0006)
school persistence	0.0217***
	(0.0023)
fuel exports	0.00695***
	(0.0012)
ores and metals exports	−0.00537***
	(0.0016)
constant	3.592***
	(0.1430)
N	383
adj. R-sq	0.903
Standard errors in parentheses	

* p<0.10, ** p<0.05, *** p<0.01

persistence can simply be mandated or prohibited by a government regardless of the quality of domestic competition, international competition or property rights protection. So, we instead use school persistence as a control in our productivity function to control for differences in human capital stock. In reality, for a particular country, it is likely that improving the regulatory environment may provide a new path to improve education where necessary. Because the pattern across all countries is ambiguous, we treat school persistence as a control.

Each factor influencing GDP is itself influenced by policy and these policies determine the scores a country receives for domestic competition, international competition and property rights protection. Therefore, we estimate the impact of the three policy scores on the productivity factors using the following regressions:

$$\begin{aligned}\log FDI\ stock = {} & \alpha_{fdi0} + \alpha_{fdi1} * Property\ rights + \alpha_{fdi2} \\ & * Domestic\ competition + \alpha_{fdi3} \\ & * International\ Cometition + \alpha_{fdi4} \\ & * (Property\ rights * domestic\ comp) + \alpha_{fdi5} \\ & * (Property\ rights * interntional\ comp) + \alpha_{fdi6} \\ & * (domestic\ comp * international\ comp) + \alpha_{fdi7} \\ & * (Property\ rights \\ & * domestic\ competition * international\ competition)\end{aligned}$$

$$\begin{aligned}\text{Healh expenditure per cap} = {} & \alpha_{health0} + \alpha_{health1} \\ & * Property\ rights + \alpha_{health2} \\ & * Domestic\ competition + \alpha_{health3} \\ & * International\ Cometition + \alpha_{health4} \\ & * (Property\ rights * domestic\ comp) + \alpha_{health5} \\ & * (Property\ rights * interntional\ comp) + \alpha_{health6} \\ & * (domestic\ comp * international\ comp) + \alpha_{health7} \\ & * (Property\ rights * domestic\ competition \\ & * international\ competition)\end{aligned}$$

$$\begin{aligned}\text{Domestic credit stock} = {} & \alpha_{dcs0} + \alpha_{dcs1} * Property\ rights + \alpha_{dcs2} \\ & * Domestic\ competition + \alpha_{dcs3} \\ & * International\ Cometition + \alpha_{dcs4} \\ & * (Property\ rights * domestic\ comp) + \alpha_{dcs5} \\ & * (Property\ rights * interntional\ comp) + \alpha_{dcs6} \\ & * (domestic\ comp * international\ comp) + \alpha_{dcs7} \\ & * (Property\ rights * domestic\ competition \\ & * international\ competition)\end{aligned}$$

In each function, the only variables entering are the scores for the three policy areas. These scores enter the equations alone and multiplied with other scores. The multiplications represent the interaction effects from changing each score included in the interaction. The coefficients on the scores by themselves represent the change in the dependent variable when that particular score changes and the other scores equal zero. For the interactions, the coefficient represents the effect on the dependent variable of changing at least one score while the other score or scores remain constant – and greater than zero – or of changing all scores in the interaction. If none of the scores for a country equals zero, then the effect of changing one score on the dependent variable will be the total of the individual effect plus all the interaction effects containing the score that is changing. Changing the score for any of the policy categories will impact each dependent variable through the total effect of the interactions and the solo effect. The results of the OLS regressions above are given in Table 3.2.

It is important to remember that the effects of changing a score in one policy are equal to the total effect from each component of the regression. So, a negative coefficient should not be seen as a negative impact on the dependent variable from improving a score, but should be seen as reducing the positive impact of the effect from the change somewhere else in the regression. This portion of the model explains between 49.4 per cent and 63.4 per cent of the variation in the factors effecting productivity.

This level of accuracy is much greater than other comparable indicators, such as the World Economic Forum's Global Competitiveness Indicators, which have an accuracy of about 19 per cent when used to predict GDP per capita. That is, when using the WEF's own indicators in the regression structure they suggest, the regression has a mean absolute prediction error of about 19 per cent. This is likely because the WEF's GCI indicator is a single value that is meant to capture the overall competitiveness of a country and, therefore, the indicator generates a weighted average of very different types of variables (such as cost of terrorism and telephony, as an example). Also, the WEF indicator includes many variables, which are the direct result of the competitive environment, as opposed to characteristics of a pro-competitive environment. Finally, the WEF suggests a very simple linear regression that directly estimates the change in GDP per capita through the GCI score and GDP growth. This fails to capture the fact that changing policy does not increase GDP directly (i.e. removing a distortion is only productivity enhancing because it allows participants in the market to optimise their behaviour, not because the policy itself is productive). Our model is much more streamlined and parsimonious than other models, and is different from other models because of the importance it ascribes to competition, which is partly why it is more accurate.

Table 3.2

	log FDI stock	*Health expenditures*	*Domestic credit stock*
Property Rights	−0.652	−3463.2***	−169.5***
	(0.98)	(1059.50)	(39.85)
International Competition	−3.011***	−15.02	−133.5***
	(0.71)	(611.60)	(22.51)
Domestic Competition	−4.845***	−1498.4**	−129.8***
	(0.74)	(631.30)	(20.82)
Property Rights * Domestic Competition	0.475**	792.0***	39.13***
	(0.24)	(280.00)	(9.08)
Property Rights * International Competition	0.374*	496.5**	52.55***
	(0.21)	(245.70)	(9.64)
Domestic * International	1.020***	−115.1	28.68***
	(0.16)	(147.80)	(4.91)
Property Rights * domestic * International	−0.111**	−59.81	−9.895***
	(0.05)	(58.74)	(1.89)
constant	19.17***	6186.5***	535.6***
	(2.63)	(2194.00)	(78.99)
N	807	803	774
adj. R-sq	0.634	0.623	0.493
Standard errors in parentheses			

* p<0.10** p<0.05*** p<0.01

To determine the impact of improving a score in one or more policy areas on GDP per capita, we find the impact of changing that score on each of the three policy areas above and then calculate the impact of that change in each of the three areas above on GDP per capita. For example, if property rights protection increases by 1, domestic competition equals 4 and international competition equals 3, then the log of FDI stock will increase by 1.038, Health expenditures will increase by 476.58 and domestic credit stock will increase by 25.93. These increases will then increase the log of GDP per capita by 0.55, which is equivalent to a 70 per cent increase in productivity.

We discounted an approach that would estimate the equations for FDI stock, domestic credit stock and health expenditures, using the fitted values from these estimates as the values in the regression on the log of GDP per capita, because the goal for this process is to find the impact of changing the policy area scores on GDP per capita. Since this is not a direct effect, we need a production function that would accurately estimate the log of GDP per capita using independent variables that are influenced by the policy area scores. We then estimate functions for FDI stock, domestic credit stock and health expenditures that are functions of the policy area scores and where the policy areas were statistically significantly influential and where the function as a whole was statistically significant. The functions did not need pin-point accuracy, but the coefficients on each policy area and the interactions needed to be accurate. This we have accomplished.

The weights used in calculating the values for property rights, domestic competition, and international competition were found by optimising an estimating equation using the statistical analysis program STATA. First, each of our available data points from the World Bank and the World Economic Forum's Global Competitiveness Indicator databases was divided into subcategories within the three competition policy areas (property rights protection, domestic competition and international competition). Using the estimating equations of FDI stock as a function of property rights, domestic competition, and international competition; health expenditures as a function of property rights, domestic competition and international competition; domestic credit stock as a function of property rights, domestic competition and international competition; school persistence as a function of property rights, domestic competition and international competition; and GDP per capita as a function of FDI stock, domestic credit stock, health expenditures per capita and school persistence, we determined the weights that would optimise the predictive power of the set of estimating equations.[52]

We assigned a random weight to each potential indicator in each subcategory and a weight for each subcategory in each policy area. Then, the equations for FDI stock, domestic credit stock, health expenditures and school persistence were estimated using OLS regressions. The fitted (or predicted) values for each regression were then used to estimate the regression for GDP per capita. The mean absolute prediction error was calculated as a percent of GDP per capita. Then, the program assigned a new weight to each value and subcategory, re-ran the regressions and then predicted GDP per capita using the new fitted values. We repeated this process to minimise the distance between the mean absolute prediction error and perfect predictive power (0 prediction error). The resulting weights predicted GDP increases with 93 per cent accuracy, using the simple regression set-up, and now predict with GDP increases with 96 per cent accuracy using the current framework. See Appendix A for the structure of the index and the weights for each subcategory and variable within the subcategories.

Using our model, we want to answer the following questions:

1. Which policies influence productivity?
2. How important is each type of policy relative to all other types in determining productivity?
3. If we solve for ACMDs in a country, what will happen to productivity?

The answer to question 3 can be found by changing the appropriate variables within the subcategories of each policy area. For example, if a country plans to make its workforce more flexible by allowing dismissal due to redundancy and we want to know what effect this will have on productivity (question 3), then the value for "Dismissal due to redundancy allowed by law?" variable in the "Ease of Recruitment and Letting Go" subcategory of the "Labour" subcategory of domestic competition will be changed from 0 to 6. Then the domestic competition score can be recalculated using the change in weighted value of "Ease of Recruitment and Letting Go" and the corresponding change in "Labour". The change in this value can be used to predict the change in stock of foreign direct investment, stock of capital provided by the financial sector and health expenditures from improving this labour regulation. These changes can then be used to predict the change in GDP per capita, giving us a predicted impact on productivity from removing an ACMD.

The answers to questions 1 and 2 can be found within the weightings themselves. The subcategories and variables within those subcategories with the greatest weights have the greatest influence on productivity (question 1). The size of the weight of one subcategory within a policy area relative to another in the same policy area (or the size of one variable within a subcategory relative to another variable in the same subcategory) will tell us the relative importance of subcategories (or variables). Also, the model will tell us the real magnitude of removing ACMDs and, so, can show real-world impacts of each ACMD type and the relative size of one impact to another. Next, we will discuss some interesting results from the weightings we estimated.

3.2.7 Reflections on What the Weightings Reveal

The weightings were evaluated statistically using STATA as described earlier as well as manually to assess how the computations make sense in the real world. The weightings show that there are many areas with counterintuitive results, and other areas where the literature supports the results.

The weights within property rights protection show that intellectual property rights protection is very important. The importance of intellectual property rights protection is well documented in the literature.[53] In fact, it has been shown that intellectual property rights have a significant impact on growth even when other types of property rights are controlled for.[54] This is precisely what the weights within property rights protection show.

The domestic competition weights give a great deal of importance to labour market regulations. These types of regulations have been established as a critical component of efficiency and welfare. Pries and Rogerson (2005)[55] develop a matching model, which shows that hiring practices play a key role in allocation and that labour market policies can distort hiring practices. They then assess the impact on labour market dynamics and welfare. Alvarez and Veracierto (1999)[56] develop a search model to explore how labour market policies generate differences in labour market performance. They analyse the impact of the existence of a minimum wage, unions, firing taxes and unemployment insurance. Their results generally verify that labour market policies do have an effect on labour market performance along the lines of unemployment, labour force participation and welfare.[57]

The World Economic Forum, the Heritage Foundation and the World Bank have each developed their own index that can be used to make cross-country comparisons of regulatory environments. The World Economic Forum's Global Competitiveness Index's stated goal is "to provide insight and stimulate discussion among all stakeholders about the best strategies and policies to help countries to overcome the obstacles to improving competitiveness".[58] The Heritage Foundation's Index of Economic Freedom "documents the positive relationship between economic freedom and a variety of positive social and economic goals".[59] The World Bank's Ease of Doing Business Index ranks countries according to how conducive the regulatory environment is to business operations.[60] Each of these indicators equally weights the components within their respective indices.[61] This means that each factor is given equal importance in grading countries with respect to each of the indices' intended metric (competitiveness, economic freedom, business conducive regulations, respectively). The literature mentioned throughout this chapter and the results of the index and model presented dispute this assumed equal-weighting approach. We see areas where this assumption does not hold.

As a general rule, it would appear that the speed of processes is less important than the actual substantive outcome. The real economic and productivity gains are to be derived in areas where substantive changes as opposed to procedural changes are made. We will focus on those areas where our weightings findings are somewhat counterintuitive.

We have found the following important issues:

1. Within the area of property rights protection, the weightings include intellectual property (25 per cent), the cost of enforcement of contracts (60 per cent), the ability to challenge government regulations (80 per cent), the strength of investor protection (53 per cent) and the outcome of insolvency as opposed to its cost or duration (59 per cent). This shows that the key

elements of any mechanism for reform at the local or national level must involve these areas to have any efficaciousness.

2. In the case of insolvency, the fact that the outcome is so critical means the major issue associated with insolvency is whether firms can be restructured or not. In other words, the speed of insolvency is not a significant factor in the economic development of changes to the insolvency rule.
3. The very high weighting (80 per cent) associated with the ability to challenge government regulations is particularly instructive. This coupled with investor protection suggests that where it is difficult to challenge government regulations, investors' rights, contract rights and property rights are also weak. This also suggests that when a government knows that it can be challenged it is less likely to violate property rights.
4. Within domestic competition, the competitiveness of the labour market is the most important factor (40 per cent). The regulatory promulgation process is also a major contributor (23 per cent). Lack of competition in infrastructure is a 20 per cent contributor. Within infrastructure, the cost of electricity is a very large factor (78 per cent) within the energy sector (itself a 30 per cent contributor within infrastructure), and financial services is a very big factor within infrastructure (a 45 per cent contributor at the level of general infrastructure). One key discovery is the fact that the weightings illustrate that government ACMDs are more of a distortion in the domestic competition area than private anti-competitive practices. This is something that has been talked about in the literature.[62] While many have suggested that government restraints are important, this is not borne out by antitrust agency practice, which is focused almost exclusively on private restraints, why lip service is paid to government restraints.
5. Within international competition, the weighting results are also important. The weightings for trade facilitation type issues (such as ease of exports and so forth) is much higher (at 52 per cent) contributor than tariffs and NTBs, which account for 35 per cent. This suggests that, during a time when tariff and NTBs are being reduced around the world, all other factors affecting the ease with which goods flow between countries are becoming increasingly important. It may also mean that countries have turned to these procedural aspects of trade policy to generate the desired outcomes they used to be able to generate with tariffs and NTBs.

3.3 Conclusion

We have contrasted the estimation of the welfare impact of ACMDs through complex econometric approaches with the use of a simpler alternative "Productivity Simulator" that focuses on nationwide measures of domestic competition, international competition and property rights protection. The two models may converge so that the alternative model may help with understanding welfare losses ordinarily derived from a welfare model. The alternative model uses loss of productivity as a proxy for welfare loss and is therefore much easier to deploy for developing country competition agencies than the standard econometric analysis. This could therefore be helpful for domestic competition agencies and others as a way of developing an understanding of ACMDs and their effects. Future research will focus on bringing these two approaches together, improving the underlying data to include only policy indicators, and trying to better understand why the weights look the way they do.

A striking feature of the results of both of our models is the importance of micro-economic factors in our estimates of productivity increases. While most policymakers focus their attention on the large fiscal and macro-economic policy tools at their disposal, these micro-economic factors are largely ignored. An important example of this was the Washington Consensus,[63] which did not really engage with the specifics of building competitive markets by reference to welfare effects. Arguably, this was one of the reasons why the first generation of reforms, which were related to open trade and property rights (to some extent), were much more successfully realised than building competitive markets inside the border. The lack of progress here has led to the highly distorted world in which we now live.

Further research is needed to deepen the factors used in the SRB Alternative model (to make them even more quantitative) and to further deepen the SRB model to produce welfare impacts in a manner that makes it easier for policymakers to use in legislative and regulatory promulgation.

Notes

1 These have been introduced in Singham and Abbott, Trade, Competition and Domestic Regulatory Policy as well as the e-resource available at: Further-Refinements-and-Developments-of-ACMD-Economic-Model2.pdf.

2 As proposed and argued in Singham, Shanker. (2007). *A General Theory of Trade and Competition: Trade Liberalisation and Competitive Markets*. Cameron May, and Singham, Shanker, and Abbott, Alden F. (2023). *Trade, Competition and Domestic Regulatory Policy*. Routledge; International competition is way of describing the openness of a country's trade regime.

3 Furubotn, Eirik G., and Pejovich, Svetozar. (1972, December). Property Rights and Economic Theory: A Survey of the Recent Literature. *Journal of Economic Literature* 10(4), 1137–1162.

4 Besley, Timothy. (1995, October). Property Rights and Investment Incentives: Theory and Evidence from Ghana. *The Journal of Political Economy* 103(5), 903–937.

5 A lack of property rights protection creates what De Soto calls "dead capital" – the poor cannot leverage the assets they do accumulate, which prevents entrepreneurialism. See Soto, Hernando De. (2000). *The Mystery*

of Capital: Why Capitalism Triumphs in the West and Fails Everywhere Else. New York: Basic. Print.

6 For a detailed treatment of the importance of intellectual property rights, see chapter 9 of: Singham, Shanker. (2007). *A General Theory of Trade and Competition: Trade Liberalisation and Competitive Markets*. Kent: Cameron May.

7 Either financially or through time commitments.

8 That is, Heritage Foundation describes why a country receives each level of score and this, in turn, provides a framework for the aspects of policy which we considered in building our indicator, available at: http://www.heritage.org/index/property-rights.

9 Porter, Michael E. (1990). *The Competitive Advantage of Nations*. New York: Free Press. As cited in Sakakibara, Mariko, and Porter, Michael E. (2001, May). Competing at Home to Win Abroad: Evidence from Japanese Industry. *The Review of Economics and Statistics* 83(2), 310–322. Positive externalities include "supplier availability, easier access to technology and market information, and specialized human resource development" (Sakakibara et al. p. 310).

10 As part of our domestic competition indicator, we include an indicator of the success of policy in limiting the ability of private entities to restrict competition through the "Effectiveness of Anti-Monopoly Policy" variable in the "Industrial Organization Regulation" subcategory.

11 Muris, Timothy J. (2005, Winter). Principles for a Successful Competition Agency. *University of Chicago Law Review* 72(1), 165–187; George Mason Law & Economics Research Paper No. 06–24, available at: SSRN: http://ssrn.com/ abstract=90167.

12 Similarly, the Washington Consensus includes privatization as one of the ten key areas of development because of the belief that that "private industry is managed more efficiently than state enterprises, because of the more direct incentives faced by a manager who either has a direct personal stake in the profits of an enterprise or else is accountable to those who do. At the very least, the threat of bankruptcy places a floor under the inefficiency of private enterprises, whereas many state enterprises seem to have unlimited access to subsidies". This theory is the backbone of our domestic competition indicator. However, regulation of private markets is not discussed in the Washington Consensus. We correct this oversight by emphasising the importance of policies which allow firms to make their own decisions. Originally conceived in: Williamson, John. (1990, April). What Washington Means by Policy Reform. Chapter 2 from *Latin American Adjustment: How Much Has Happened?* Ed. John Williamson, available at: http://iie.com/publications/papers/paper.cfm?ResearchID=486 See also: http://www.who.int/trade/glossary/ story094/en/

http://www.economicshelp.org/blog/7387/economics/washington-consensus-definition-and-criticism/

http: //www.piie.com/publications/chapters_preview/6628/02iie6628.pdf

13 When changing market characteristics, such as new technologies, eliminate natural monopoly conditions, however, maintaining government regulation may become counterproductive and welfare-inimical, and such regulation should be lifted.

14 Before the government acts, care should be taken to ensure that the private sector cannot adequately rectify the market failure at issue, and that the costs associated with government intervention are not likely to outweigh the benefits that flow from eliminating (or reducing) the market failure.
15 The welfare-maximising number and size of firms will depend on the market (type of good, substitutes, demand, etc.)
16 The ideal infrastructure measures would be those that reflect the policy for awarding contracts for infrastructure projects (specifically, for building, managing or maintaining infrastructure). However, the primary data available are concerned with outcomes, with only a couple of exceptions in financial infrastructure.
17 For a description of the theory, see: Bajona, Claustre, Gibson, Mark J., Kehoe, Timothy J., and Ruhl, Kim J. (2008). *Trade Liberalization, Growth, and Productivity*. Prepared for the Conference "New Directions in International Trade Theory" at the University of Nottingham, available at: http://www.econ.umn.edu/~tkehoe/papers/BajonaGibsonKehoeRuhl.pdf.

Note: These authors also highlight the fact that trade openness does not always lead to increased GDP and that the theory does not predict an increase in GDP from openness. The theory does predict greater welfare from openness, though. We will use GDP per capita as our proxy for welfare because we do not have a direct measure of welfare. There are many sources which do find a positive relationship between openness and GDP. A few examples include (as cited in Bajona et al. (2010)): Frankel, J. A., and Romer, D. (1999). Does Trade Cause Growth? *American Economic Review* 89, 379–399. Hall, R., and Jones, C. (1999). Why Do Some Countries Produce So Much More Output Per Worker Than Others? *Quarterly Journal of Economics* 114, 83–116. Alcalá, F., and Ciccone, A. (2004). Trade and Productivity. *Quarterly Journal of Economics* 119, 613–646.
18 *Economics*, 119, 613–646. Williamson, John. (1990, April). What Washington Means by Policy Reform. Chapter 2 from *Latin American Adjustment: How Much Has Happened?* Ed. John Williamson, available at: http://iie.com/publications/papers/paper.cfm? ResearchID=486.
19 Though, again, no emphasis was given to the competitive environment within a country except for the stress on privatisation.
20 See SRB (2014).
21 Source: http://unctadstat.unctad.org/wds/ReportFolders/reportFolders.aspx?sRF_ActivePath=p,5&sRF_Expanded=,p,5.
22 Source for health expenditures per cap, domestic credit stock, school persistence, fuel exports and ore and metal exports: http://databank.worldbank.org/data/home.aspx.
23 Solow, Robert M. (2001). What Have We Learned from a Decade of Empirical Research on Growth? Applying Growth Theory across Countries. *The World Bank Economic Review* 15(2), 283–288, available at: https://doi.org/10.1093/wber/15.2.283.
24 *Economic factors* includes things like "size of the government", "openness of the economy", etc.; *Institutions* includes things like "political stability", "democratic rights", etc.; *Social base* includes things like "ethnic and religious composition of the population", etc.; *Physical base* includes things like "location of a country", "climate", "access to sea", etc.

Source: Islam, Nazrul. (2005, October). *Determinants of Productivity: A Two-Stage Analysis*. Working Paper Series 2005–13. International Centre for the Study of East Asian Development.

25 Solow, Robert M. (1956, February). A Contribution to the Theory of Economic Growth. *The Quarterly Journal of Economics* 70(1), 65–94.

26 Total factor productivity (TFP) has been shown to be a key component of productivity as well (for example: Solow, Robert M. (1957, August). Technical Change and the Aggregate Production Function. *Review of Economics and Statistics* 39, 312–320; Denison, Edward F. (1985). *Trends in American Economic Growth, 1929–1982*. Washington: Brookings Institution; Jones, Charles I. (1997, Summer). On the Evolution of the World Income Distribution. *Journal of Economic Perspectives* 11, 19–36.). TFP is typically measured as the Solow residual, which would be the residual in our model. Our concern here is estimating the effect of removing ACMDs on GDP through the effect of reducing ACMDs on capital and labour. This is essentially the first step in the process of using the ACMD index to evaluate the impact of ACMDs. Future research should attempt to disaggregate the types of inputs (capital, labour and TFP) to find the specific way in which ACMDs reduce productivity and welfare.

27 Numerous studies show this relationship. A few examples include:

Barro, Robert J. (1991, May). Economic Growth in a Cross Section of Countries. *Quarterly Journal of Economics*. May, 1991.

Mauro, Paolo. (1995, August). Corruption and Growth. *Quarterly Journal of Economics*.

Besley, Timothy. (1995, October). Property Rights and Investment Incentives: Theory and Evidence from Ghana. *The Journal of Political Economy* 103(5), 903–937.

Svensson, Jakob. (1998).Investment, Property Rights, and Political Stability. *European Economic Review* 42, 1317–1341.

28 See, for example: Levine, Ross, Loayza, Norman, and Beck, Thorsten. (2000). Financial Intermediation and Growth: Causality and Causes. *Journal of Monetary Economics* 46.

Levine, Ross, and Zervos, Sara. (1998, June). Stock Markets, Banks, and Economic Growth. *The American Economic Review*.

29 Zagha, Roberto, and Nankani, Gobind T. (eds.). (2005). *Economic Growth in the 1990s: Learning from a Decade of Reform*. Chapter 7. World Bank Publications.

30 Aiyar, Shekhar, and Jain-Chandra, Sonali. (2012). *The Domestic Credit Supply Response to International Bank Deleveraging: Is Asia Different?* IMF Working Paper WP/12/258. Asia and Pacific Department. IMF.

31 Williamson, John. (1990, April). "What Washington Means by Policy Reform." Chapter 2 from *Latin American Adjustment: How Much Has Happened?* Ed. John Williamson, available at: http://iie.com/publications/papers/paper.cfm?ResearchID=486.

32 Adams, Samuel. (2010, July). Intellectual Property Rights, Investment Climate, and FDI in Developing Countries. *International Business Research* 3(3).

33 Adams (2010) shows that patent protection had a greater, positive influence on FDI after the adoption of TRIPS, which tells us that committing

to protecting intellectual property and actually increasing patent protection together attracted more FDI.

34 Ramamurti, Ravi, and Doh, John P. (2004). Rethinking Foreign Infrastructure Investment in Developing Countries. *Journal of World Business* 39.

35 Lucas, Jr., Robert E. (1990, May). Why Doesn't Capital Flow from Rich to Poor Countries? *The American Economic Review* 80(2), 92–96.

36 Bayraktar, Nihal. (2013). Foreign Direct Investment and Investment Climate. *Procedia Economics and Finance* 5, 83–92.

37 Nnadozie, E., and Njuguna, A. E. (2013). *Investment Climate and Foreign Direct Investment in Africa*. Mimeo, United Nations Economic Commission for Africa.

38 Pan, Yigang et al. (2014). Firms' FDI Ownership the Influence of Government Ownership and Legislative Connections. *Journal of International Business Studies* 45.

39 Pilarska, Czeslawa, and Walega, Grzegorz. (2014, September 11–13). Determinants of FDI Inflows to Poland, Czech Republic and Hungary in Context of Integration into European Union. *The 8th International Days of Statistics and Economics, Prague.*

40 This interdependence has been documented many times. Some examples include:

Dunning, John H. (2003, Fall). The Role of Foreign Direct Investment in Upgrading China's Competitiveness. *Journal of International Business and Economics.*

United Nations Conference on Trade and Development's World Investment Reports (numerous reports, but the 1998 and 2012 report focus on trends in determinants of FDI and investment climate, political stability, and openness of trade are factors in each report).

41 The literature supports the use of health expenditures as a proxy for health outcomes: Farag, Marwa et al. (2012). Health Expenditures, Health Outcomes and the Role of Good Governance. *International Journal of Health Care Finance and Economics* 13(1), 33–52. This study shows that health expenditures reduce child and infant mortality rates in low- and middle-income countries and that good governance improve this effect; Bokhari, Farasat A. S., Gai, Yunwei, and Gottret, Pablo. (2007). Government Health Expenditures and Health Outcomes. *Health Economics* 16(3), 257–273. This study shows that health expenditures reduce infant and maternal mortality rates across all income levels; Anyanwu, John C., and Erhijakpor, Andrew E. O. (2007). *Health Expenditures and Health Outcomes in Africa*. Working Paper No. 91. African Development Bank. This study shows that the relationship between health expenditures and child and infant mortality rates holds for Africa; Joumard, I., Andre, C., and Nicq, C. (2010). *Health Care Systems: Efficiency and Institutions*. OECD Economics Department Working Papers, No. 769. OECD Publishing, Paris. This study shows that 40 per cent of the increase in life-expectancy since 1990 for OECD countries can be attributed to increases in health expenditures.

42 Cockburn, Iain M. (2009). Intellectual Property Rights and Pharmaceuticals: Challenges and Opportunities for Economic Research. *The Economics of Intellectual Property*, Chapter 5, World Intellectual Property Organization, Geneva.
43 Berndt, Ernst R., Blalock, Nathan, and Cockburn, Iain M. (2011). Diffusion of New Drugs In The Post-TRIPS Era. *International Journal of the Economics of Business* 18(2), 203–224.
44 Berndt et al. (2011).
45 Gaynor, Martin, and Town, Robert J. (2011, July). *Competition in Health Care Markets*. NBER Working Paper 17208.
46 Waeger, Patricia. (2007). *Trade in Health Services: An Analytical Framework*. Kiel Advanced Studies Working Papers, No. 441.
47 U.S. International Trade Commission. (2013). *Recent Trends in U.S. Services Trade – Annual Report.*
48 Middle East and Central Asia Department. (2014, May). *Regional Economic Outlook Update*. International Monetary Fund.
49 Harb, N. (2009). Oil Exports, Non-Oil GDP, and Investment in the GCC Countries. *Review of Development Economics* 13, 695–708.
50 Davis, Graham A. (2010, January). *Trade in Mineral Resources: Background Paper to the 2010 World Trade Report*. World Trade Organization: Economic Statistics and Research Division. Staff Working Paper ESRD-2010–01.
51 Many studies have examined the relationship between education and productivity or wages. Some examples include:

Duflo, Esther. (2001). Schooling and Labor Market Consequences of School Construction in Indonesia: Evidence from an Unusual Policy Experiment. *American Economic Review* 91(4), 795–813.

Rosenzweig, M. (1995). Why Are There Returns to Schooling. *American Economic Review* 85(2), 153–158.

Ashenfelter, Orley, and Alan Krueger. (1994). Estimates of the Economic Return to Schooling from a New Sample of Twins. *American Economic Review* 84(5), 1157–1173.
52 We used this specification to calculate the weights because we were trying to maximise the correlation between the three policy areas and productivity through the factors directly affecting productivity. After the weights were determined, we revisited the model and came to the specification used here.
53 See Singham (2007) and the following examples:

Khoury, Theodore A., and Peng, Mike W. (2011). Does Institutional Reform of Intellectual Property Rights Lead to More Inbound FDI? Evidence from Latin America and the Caribbean. *Journal of World Business* 46.

Eicher, Theo, and Garcia-Penalosa, Cecilia. (2008). Endogenous Strength of Intellectual Property Rights_ Implications for Economic Development and Growth. *European Economic Review* 52.

Iwaisako, Tatsuro, Tanaka, Hitoshi, and Futagami, Koichi. (2011). A Welfare Analysis of Global Patent Protection in a Model with

Endogenous Innovation and Foreign Direct Investment. *European Economic Review* 55.

Tanaka, Hitoshi, and Iwaisako, Tatsuro. (2014). Intellectual Property Rights and Foreign Direct Investment. *European Economic Review* 67.

54 Park, Walter G., and Ginarte, Juan Carlos. (1997, July). Intellectual Property Rights and Economic Growth. *Contemporary Economic Policy* XV.

55 Pries, Michael, and Rogerson, Richard. (2005). Hiring Policies, Labor Market Institutions, and Labor Market Flows. *Journal of Political Economy* 113(4).

56 Alvarez, Fernando, and Veracierto, Marcelo. (1999). Labor-Market Policies in an Equilibrium Search Model. *NBER Macroeconomics Annual* 14. Ed. Ben Bernanke and Julio Rotemberg.

57 The authors also compare their results with the existing empirical studies and find that the empirical literature is generally in agreement.

58 World Economic Forum. (2014). *Global Competitiveness 2014–2015.* Geneva: World Economic Forum.

59 http://www.heritage.org/index/about.

60 http://data.worldbank.org/indicator/IC.BUS.EASE.XQ.

61 The GCI is the only exception because it shifts weights among the broadest categories depending on the income level of the country it is ranking. However, the variables within the subcategories within the "pillars" of these broad categories all have equal weights, as do the subcategories, as do the pillars. The broadest categories relate to the types of production an economy can pursue and the weights are greatest within each income level for the types of production a country at that level of development is most likely to pursue. In this way, the GCI takes equally weighted variables and weights them in such a way as to fit the score of a country to its relative level of income. So, lower-income countries will get lower scores and higher-income countries will get higher scores by construction.

62 See, for example: Muris, Timothy J. (2005, Winter). Principles for a Successful Competition Agency. *University of Chicago Law Review* 72(1), 165–187; George Mason Law & Economics Research Paper No. 06–24, available at: SSRN: http://ssrn.com/abstract=901677;

Muris, Timothy J. (2003). Looking Forward: The Federal Trade Commission and the Future Development of U.S. Competition Policy. *Columbia Business Law Review* 359, 363.

63 Williamson, John (1990).

4 Recent Improvements, and Refinements of Singham-Rangan-Bradley model and Introduction to Probabilistic Analysis of the Quantum of Distortion[1]

4.1 Changes to SRB Model

The issues which have been raised by the SRB model above are principally related to endogeneity concerns.

Initial projections from the SRB model suggest that a reduction in anti-competitive market distortions (ACMDs) does lead to a significant increase in GDP per capita in line with the projections from the agency-based model and from other sources, such as OECD and other figures on the impact of anti-competitive regulation on growth.

In order to deal with the concerns which emanate from attempting a single correlation between a single pillar score covering IC, DC and PR, we then attempted to break down each pillar or force to correlate that force with GDP per capita by itself. We found that this eliminated the endogeneity concern. We also greatly simplified the model specifications as below.

$$\ln(GDP\ per\ capita)_{it} = \beta_0 + \beta_1 Domestic\ competition_{it} + \boldsymbol{X}_{it}'\gamma + v_t + \lambda_i + \in_{it}$$

$$\ln(GDP\ per\ capita)_{it} = \beta_0 + \beta_1 Peoperty\ Rights_{it} + \boldsymbol{X}_{it}'\gamma + v_t + \lambda_i + \in_{it}$$

$$\ln(GDP\ per\ capita)_{it} = \beta_0 + \beta_1 International\ competition_{it} + \boldsymbol{X}_{it}'\gamma + v_t + \lambda_i + \in_{it}$$

We construct a panel data model of GDP as a function of each competition index, several observed control variables and an unobserved time-invariant country-specific effect and a country-invariant time period-specific effect. Below, we discuss these variables.

DOI: 10.4324/9781003570608-4

4.2 Variables

4.2.1 GDP Per Capita

GDP per capita data are used in 2017 international dollar PPP terms (sourced from IMF World Economic Outlook) to enable comparison between countries. This variable is logged. This means we can interpret the coefficients in terms of percentage changes.

4.2.2 Modification to Indices

Central to the modelling approach is the use of the indices developed in Singham, Rangan, Bradley and Kiniry.[2] These data have been updated for each index and, where publications have been discontinued, we have used alternative sources, which essentially measure similar aspects of competition.

The updated sources and weights are given in Table 4.1.

Domestic Competition:

Table 4.1 Domestic Competition Index Sources and Weights

Sub index	*Source*	*Weights*
Labour freedom score		
Minimum wage	Index of Economic Freedom	25.0%
Associational right		
Paid annual leave		
Notice period for redundancy dismissal		
Severance pay for redundancy dismissal		
Labour productivity		
Labour force participation rate		
Restrictions on overtime work		
Redundancy dismissal permitted by law		
Business freedom score		
Access to electricity	Index of Economic Freedom	25.0%
Business environment risk		
Regulatory quality		
Women's economic inclusion		
Financial freedom score		
The extent of government regulation of financial services	Index of Economic Freedom	6.3%
The degree of state intervention in banks and other financial firms through direct and indirect ownership		
Government influence on the allocation of credit		
The extent of financial and capital market development		
Openness to foreign competition		

(*Continued*)

Table 4.1 (Continued)

Sub index	*Source*	*Weights*
Electricity cost	WB Doing Business	3.1%
Electricity time	WB Doing Business	3.1%
Quality of roads 1–7	Global Competitiveness Index	3.1%
Quality of ports 1–5	Logistics Performance Index	3.1%
Mobile telephone subscription	Global Competitiveness Index	3.1%
Individuals using internet %	Global Competitiveness Index	3.1%
Government Integrity Score		
Perceptions of corruption Bribery risk Control of corruption	Index of Economic Freedom	25.0%

The domestic competition index is a composite one made up of the sub-indices shown earlier. The sub-indices from the index of economic freedom take into account the following factors:

- **Business Freedom**

The business freedom component measures the extent to which a country's regulatory and infrastructure environments constrain the efficient operation of businesses. The quantitative score is derived from an array of factors that affect **the ease of starting, operating and closing a business**. The business freedom score for each country is a number between 0 and 100, with 100 indicating the freest business environment. It is based on four equally weighted sub-factors:

- Access to electricity
- Business environment risk
- Regulatory quality
- Women's economic inclusion.

- **Labour Freedom**

The labour freedom component is a quantitative measure that considers various aspects of the legal and regulatory framework of a country's labour market. The score for the labour freedom component is based on nine equally weighted sub-factors:

- Minimum wage
- Associational right

- Paid annual leave
- Notice period for redundancy dismissal
- Severance pay for redundancy dismissal
- Labour productivity
- Labour force participation rate
- Restrictions on overtime work
- Redundancy dismissal permitted by law

- **Financial Freedom**

Financial freedom is both an indicator of banking efficiency and a measure of independence from government control and interference in the financial sector.

To assess the overall level of financial freedom that ensures easy and effective access to financing opportunities for people and businesses in a country's economy, the index takes account of five broad areas:

- The extent of government regulation of financial services
- The degree of state intervention in banks and other financial firms through direct and indirect ownership
- Government influence on the allocation of credit
- The extent of financial and capital market development
- Openness to foreign competition

Government Integrity

The score for this component is derived by averaging scores for three equally weighted sub-factors:

- Perceptions of corruption
- Bribery risk and
- Control of corruption including "capture" of the state by elites and private interests

4.2.3 International Competition

- The LPI timeliness indicator measures the frequency with which shipments reach consignees within schedules or expected delivery times from hardly ever to nearly always.
- The international shipment indicator measures the ease of arranging competitively priced shipments from very difficult to very easy.
- The LPI customs indicator measures the efficiency of customs and border management clearance from very low to very high.

- The trade freedom score is a composite measure of the extent of tariff and non-tariff barriers that affect imports and exports of goods and services. The trade freedom score is based on two inputs, the trade-weighted average tariff rate and a qualitative evaluation of non-tariff barriers (NTBs).

4.2.4 Property Rights

- Efficiency of legal framework in challenging regulations is a score based on responses to the survey question on the ease for private businesses to challenge government actions and/or regulations through the legal system (1 = extremely difficult; 7 = extremely easy). This is sourced from the World Economic Forum, Executive Opinion Survey.
- Efficiency of legal framework in settling disputes is a score based on responses to the survey question on how efficient are the legal and judicial systems for companies in settling disputes (1 = extremely inefficient; 7 = extremely efficient). This is sourced from the World Economic Forum, Executive Opinion Survey.
- Intellectual property protection is a score based on the response to the survey question "In your country, to what extent is intellectual property protected?" (1 = not at all; 7 = to a great extent). This is sourced from the World Economic Forum, Executive Opinion Survey.
- Strength of minority investor protection measures the strength of minority shareholder protections against misuse of corporate assets by directors for their personal gain, as well as shareholder rights, governance safeguards and corporate transparency requirements that reduce the risk of abuse.
- The strength of legal rights index measures the degree to which collateral and bankruptcy laws protect the rights of borrowers and lenders and thus facilitate lending.
- Judicial independence is a score based on responses to the survey question on how independent the judicial system is from influences of the government, individuals or companies (1 = not independent at all; 7 = entirely independent). This is sourced from the World Economic Forum, Executive Opinion Survey.
- The enforcing contracts indicators measure the time and cost for resolving a commercial dispute through a local first-instance court.
- The registering property indicators examine the steps, time and cost involved in registering a property, assuming a standardised case of an entrepreneur who wanted to purchase land and a building that were already registered and free of title dispute.
- The resolving insolvency indicators measure the time, cost and outcome of insolvency proceedings involving domestic legal entities.

4.2.5 Expected Years of Schooling

Expected years of schooling will proxy human capital. Human capital is emphasised to varying degrees by different strands of economic growth literature as a determinant of a country's income. We control for it as we suspect it is systematically related to our indices of interest and would hence bias any estimate. These data are taken from the World Bank.

4.2.6 Population (Log)

The growth literature has also raised the possibility of "scale" effects in determining a country's income. To avoid bias through the mechanism detailed earlier, we will control for the size of the economy in terms of population. Source: IMF World Economic Outlook

4.2.7 Fiscal Expenditure as a Percentage of GDP

Fiscal stimulus may contemporaneously impact GDP and be systematically related to our index of choice. This variable is therefore introduced to eliminate this possible bias in estimation. These data are taken from the IMF fiscal monitor.

4.2.8 Other Controls Tested

The findings presented herein are robust to a range of different controls not included in the main model. These include natural resources rent, life expectancy and percentage of population of working age.

4.2.9 Time and Country Dummies

There are likely factors that impact a country's income that we have not included in our model. If they are systematically related to our index of interest, this will bias our estimates. We can take steps to minimise this risk by introducing **time and country dummy variables**.

These will capture the time-invariant country effects, λ_i, and country-invariant time effects, ν_t, specified in equations (1–3). An example of a time-invariant country effects might be omitted institutional factors, geographical factors or cultural factors that impact the level of income. An example of a country-invariant time effect is a global trend such as oil prices. It is plausible that our indices are correlated with these factors. If this is the case, then our coefficient of interest will be biased by their omission. A country dummy variable eliminates this source of bias, as we only attribute variance in income to varying factors inside a country that cannot be explained by global trends.

The drawback of this is that these dummy variables will "soak up" large amounts of the variation in the sample, which makes estimation harder. Hence, estimation has been carried out without dummy variables, with just time dummy variables, with just country dummy variables and with both dummy variables. This lets us look at both sides of this trade-off bias/variance trade-off in estimation.

4.3 Limitations of the Model

4.3.1 Time-Varying Unobserved Country Heterogeneity

A potential limitation of this approach is that even with time and country dummy variables, unobserved time-varying country effects may confound estimates. We could deal with this by introducing time and country interaction terms; however, this generates an infeasible number of parameters to estimate given the panel data available.

4.3.2 Reverse Causality

This model can provide evidence of pattern of association between the index of interest and a country's income that is robust to other factors. A casual interpretation of this can be made; however; any such interpretation is beyond the strict implications of this model. An index may contemporaneously cause a country's income, a country's income may contemporaneously cause an index or the two may be casually unrelated. Each of these cases would be consistent with a statistically significant coefficient on an index.

4.3.3 Lagged Effects

The potential causal mechanisms are not restricted to the contemporaneous effects. It may be that a previous year's competition policy impacts GDP in three years. Our analysis, on the other hand, is restricted to the contemporaneous effects. Missing out these lagged effects again makes it difficult to construct a causal narrative from this model. Also, this may create omitted variable biases if lags of indices are relevant to GDP and systematically related to current values of indices.

4.4 SRB-γ Model Final Refinements

To test the hypotheses, we employ the ordinary least squares estimation method. In the econometric model, the dependent variables are the natural logarithm of country annual per capita income. These models test the hypotheses that property rights, domestic competition and international competition are positively related to national per capita income. Depending on the regression model specifications, as controls, we are including country-fixed effects, year-fixed effects and within-country time-varying variables. In all regression models, we cluster the standard errors by country.[3]

The results for property rights, international competition and domestic competition are reported in Tables 4.1, 4.2 and 4.3 respectively. The results indicate that an increase in property rights is positively associated with GDP per capita (Table 4.1). As is the case for all three tables, the first column does not control for government or education, the second column controls for government, the third column controls for education and the last column controls for government and education. The coefficients on government and education, however, are not statistically significant and our preferred specification

Table 4.2 International Competition Index Sources and Weights

Sub component	*Source*	*Weights*
LPI timeliness indicator	Logistics Performance Index	11%
LPI international shipment indicator	Logistics Performance Index	36%
LPI customs indicator	Logistics Performance Index	10%
Trade Freedom score	Index of Economic Freedom	29%
Freedom of foreigners to visit	Human Freedom Index	8%
Freedom to own foreign currency	Human Freedom Index	4%
Capital controls	Human Freedom Index	1%

Table 4.3 Property Rights Index Sources and Weights

Sub-component	*Source*	*Weights*
Efficiency of the judicial system		**30%**
Efficiency of the legal framework in challenging regulations	Global Competitiveness Index	80%
Efficiency of the legal framework in settling disputes	Global Competitiveness Index	20%
Intellectual property protection	**Global Competitiveness Index**	**25%**
Integrity of the legal system		**17%**

(*Continued*)

Table 4.3 (Continued)

Sub-component	*Source*	*Weights*
Strength of minority investor protection	WB Doing Business	53%
Legal rights index (financial)	WB Doing Business	32%
Judicial independence	Global Competitiveness Index	15%
Enforcing contracts		**15%**
Enforcing contracts (cost)	WB Doing Business	60%
Registering property (cost)	WB Doing Business	20%
Enforcing contracts (time)	WB Doing Business	15%
Registering property (time)	WB Doing Business	5%
Resolving insolvency		**13%**
Outcome (0 as piecemeal sale and 1 as going concern)	WB Doing Business	59%
Time (years)	WB Doing Business	17%
Cost (% of estate)	WB Doing Business	14%
Recovery rate (cents on dollar)	WB Doing Business	10%

is column 1. Specifically, a one-unit increase in the property rights index is associated with approximately 6.6 per cent increase in GDP per capita and the results are highly significant. The R-squared value given in the table is based on within transformation, that is, the model accounts for approximately 51 per cent of the variance within the panel units (the countries).

The results for the international competition index and domestic competition index are reported in Tables 4.2 and 4.3 respectively. Our preferred specification is the first column for these models as well. Specifically, a one-unit increase in the international competition index is associated with a 2.6 per cent increase in GDP per capita, although the results are not statistically significant (Table 4.2). Finally, a one-unit increase in the domestic competition index is associated with an 11.4 per cent increase in GDP per capita and the results are highly significant (Table 4.3).

The variables and sub-variables used are available in the Growth Commission's 2023 Growth Budget[4] at pp. 72–83 (appendix 1). The datasets derived from the analysis of variables are set out in the attached excel spreadsheets (See Tables 4.4–4.6 below).

Table 4.4 Models for Property Rights Index

	lngdppc	*lngdppc*	*lngdppc*	*lngdppc*
Property rights	0.066 **	0.057 **	0.068 **	0.058 **
	(0.019)	(0.020)	(0.019)	(0.020)
year				
2011	0.025 **	0.023 **	0.023 **	0.020 **
	(0.004)	(0.005)	(0.005)	(0.005)
2012	0.042 **	0.039 **	0.039 **	0.036 **
	(0.006)	(0.006)	(0.006)	(0.006)
2013	0.062 **	0.058 **	0.056 **	0.052 **
	(0.008)	(0.008)	(0.009)	(0.008)
2014	0.085 **	0.080 **	0.078 **	0.073 **
	(0.009)	(0.009)	(0.010)	(0.009)
2015	0.101 **	0.097 **	0.093 **	0.089 **
	(0.010)	(0.010)	(0.012)	(0.011)
2016	0.113 **	0.110 **	0.104 **	0.101 **
	(0.011)	(0.012)	(0.013)	(0.012)
2017	0.139 **	0.135 **	0.129 **	0.125 **
	(0.013)	(0.013)	(0.015)	(0.014)
2018	0.161 **	0.157 **	0.150 **	0.146 **
	(0.014)	(0.014)	(0.016)	(0.015)
2019	0.174 **	0.172 **	0.162 **	0.160 **
	(0.015)	(0.015)	(0.018)	(0.017)
Gov expenditure (% of GDP)		−0.003		−0.003
		(0.002)		(0.002)
Expected Years of Schooling			0.012	0.012
			(0.010)	(0.010)
Intercept	8.477 **	8.604 **	8.296 **	8.433 **
	(0.079)	(0.120)	(0.155)	(0.171)
R-squared	0.5082	0.5233	0.5091	0.5239
Prob > F	0.0000	0.0000	0.0000	0.0000
Number of observations	1219	1116	1209	1106

** p<.01, * p<.05.

Table 4.5 Models for International Competition Index

	lngdppc	*lngdppc*	*lngdppc*	*lngdppc*
International Competition	0.026	0.016	0.026	0.016
	(0.022)	(0.022)	(0.022)	(0.022)
year				
2011	0.021 **	0.018 **	0.020 **	0.017 **
	(0.005)	(0.005)	(0.005)	(0.005)
2012	0.039 **	0.035 **	0.037 **	0.033 **
	(0.007)	(0.006)	(0.007)	(0.007)

(*Continued*)

Table 4.5 (Continued)

	lngdppc	*lngdppc*	*lngdppc*	*lngdppc*
2013	0.059 **	0.055 **	0.055 **	0.050 **
	(0.008)	(0.008)	(0.009)	(0.008)
2014	0.075 **	0.071 **	0.070 **	0.066 **
	(0.010)	(0.009)	(0.011)	(0.010)
2015	0.091 **	0.087 **	0.085 **	0.081 **
	(0.011)	(0.010)	(0.013)	(0.011)
2016	0.111 **	0.108 **	0.104 **	0.101 **
	(0.012)	(0.011)	(0.014)	(0.012)
2017	0.135 **	0.132 **	0.128 **	0.124 **
	(0.014)	(0.013)	(0.016)	(0.014)
2018	0.159 **	0.155 **	0.151 **	0.146 **
	(0.015)	(0.014)	(0.017)	(0.015)
2019	0.174 **	0.171 **	0.165 **	0.162 **
	(0.016)	(0.015)	(0.018)	(0.017)
Gov expenditure (% of GDP)		−0.003		−0.003
		(0.003)		(0.003)
Expected Years of Schooling			0.010	0.010
			(0.011)	(0.011)
Intercept	8.674 **	8.811 **	8.532 **	8.670 **
	(0.096)	(0.146)	(0.180)	(0.195)
R-squared	0.4889	0.5047	0.4882	0.5038
Prob > F	0.0000	0.0000	0.000	0.000
Number of observations	1154	1057	1144	1047

** p<.01, * p<.05

Table 4.6 Models for Domestic Competition Index

	lngdppc	*lngdppc*	*lngdppc*	*lngdppc*
Domestic Competition	0.114 **	0.099 **	0.112 **	0.097 **
	(0.030)	(0.029)	(0.030)	(0.030)
year				
2011	0.025 **	0.022 **	0.023 **	0.021 **
	(0.005)	(0.005)	(0.005)	(0.005)
2012	0.040 **	0.038 **	0.038 **	0.035 **
	(0.006)	(0.006)	(0.006)	(0.006)
2013	0.063 **	0.059 **	0.060 **	0.055 **
	(0.008)	(0.007)	(0.008)	(0.008)
2014	0.080 **	0.076 **	0.076 **	0.070 **
	(0.009)	(0.008)	(0.010)	(0.009)
2015	0.093 **	0.089 **	0.087 **	0.083 **
	(0.010)	(0.009)	(0.012)	(0.010)
2016	0.114 **	0.110 **	0.108 **	0.103 **
	(0.011)	(0.010)	(0.013)	(0.012)

(*Continued*)

Table 4.6 (Continued)

	lngdppc	*lngdppc*	*lngdppc*	*lngdppc*
2017	0.141 **	0.136 **	0.134 **	0.129 **
	(0.012)	(0.012)	(0.014)	(0.013)
2018	0.166 **	0.161 **	0.159 **	0.153 **
	(0.013)	(0.013)	(0.016)	(0.015)
2019	0.178 **	0.174 **	0.169 **	0.165 **
	(0.014)	(0.014)	(0.017)	(0.016)
Gov expenditure (% of GDP)		−0.003		−0.003
		(0.002)		(0.002)
Expected Years of Schooling			0.009	0.009
			(0.010)	(0.010)
Intercept	8.241 **	8.409 **	8.121 **	8.288 **
	(0.134)	(0.150)	(0.188)	(0.187)
R-squared	0.5213	0.5339	0.5205	0.5330
Prob > F	0.0000	0.0000	0.0000	0.0000
Number of observations	1219	1116	1209	1106

** p<.01, * p<.05

4.5 Correlation with GDP Per Capita Minus Government Spending

To stimulate economic growth, policy must stimulate private economic activity. To more closely correlate changes in the IC, DC and PR fields with this stimulation of private economic activity, we have stripped out government spending from the GDP per capita numbers.

We have also applied the model stripping out the government spending element of GDP per capita. This is appropriate, as we are trying to ascertain the impact of changing the field scores of IC, DC and PR on the generation of actual private sector economic activity. We acknowledge that as private sector economic activity increases, so do tax revenue and the potential for increased government spending. For the SRB-γ model, we see the following results.

4.6 Results

The summary statistics in Table 4.1 show that the logarithm of GDP per capita is 8.84, which translates into about $6,900 real 2017 dollars when using a purchasing price parity deflator. When government spending is removed from GDP per capita, the logarithm falls to 8.45 or about $4,675 in real 2017 dollars. Looking at the non-government share of GDP per capita can be useful in this context because it focuses on the economic activity driven by private businesses rather than government spending. The means of the domestic competition, international competition index and the property rights indices range between 4.1 and 4.5, while the theoretical maximum for each index is 7.

Table 4.2 shows the regression results from estimating the effects of each of the three indices. All specifications in Table 4.2 include country effects (indicators) and year effects (indicators). Formally, the regression equation estimated is $y_{it} = \beta_{it} X_{it} + \mu_i + \lambda_t + \varepsilon_{it}$ where the subscript *i* indicates the country, *t* the year, *y* stands for GDP per capita, X is one of our three indexes, μ represents the indicator variable included for each country, λ represents the indicators included for each year and ε is the error term.

In this regression model, year indicators adjust the estimates to take account of common annual shocks hitting all countries, such as a global financial crisis. Country indicators adjust our estimates for the differences in national institutions, political regimes and cultures, for example, which are constant and thus do not change between 2010 and 2019. Therefore, any country-level time-constant variables are accounted for in our model, and the estimated coefficients on our three indices cannot be explained by underlying country characteristics, such as their institutions, political regimes or cultures that did not change between 2010 and 2019, which is our period of analysis. The fact that we are studying a relatively short period of ten years makes the country indicators quite powerful in this modelling approach, as the concern about omitted time-varying country-level variables becomes less prominent for a shorter period, enhancing our confidence that we are estimating causal effects.

In Table 4.2, the first three columns show the regression estimates on the indices when the natural logarithm of the country's GDP per capita is the dependent variable. The last three columns show their effect on GDP per capita when government spending is removed from the GDP per capita measure.

Overall, the estimated coefficients on all three indices are positive. The domestic competition and property rights index are statistically significant in the first three columns of Table 4.2. In columns 4–5, all three estimates are statistically significant when filtering out government spending from the GDP per capita measure.

In Table 4.2, column (4), the estimate for the domestic competition variable is 0.112, indicating that a one-point increase in the domestic competition index is associated with an 11 per cent increase in GDP per capita. The estimates on international competition in column 5 indicate that a one-point increase in the international competition index is associated with a 4.4 per cent increase in GDP per capita; and a one-point increase in the property rights index is associated with a 7.3 per cent increase.

Interestingly, the estimated coefficients on international competition and the property rights index are larger in magnitude when filtering out government spending from the GDP per capita measure, as done in the last three columns of Table 4.2. The correlation between GDP per capita minus government spending and the IC pillar is more robust than GDP per capita inclusive of government spending. We acknowledge that government spending and private sector growth are somewhat correlatable, as the more tax receipts are collected from this enhanced private activity, the more governments can spend, but we do not think this is problematic because there is also an argument that, especially in developed countries, government spending and private tax receipts are somewhat decoupled due to fiscal distortions (the fiat money system itself being a primary one).

Overall, the findings are consistent with the hypothesis that greater competition – both domestic and international – and more robust property rights facilitate higher GDP per capita because they increase citizens' incentive to engage in productive activities.

To examine how sensitive our results are to alternative regression model specifications, Table 4.3 includes the time-varying control variable, which measures the annual country's educational attainment and population size (See Tables 4.7–4.9). Due to missing values for educational achievement and country population size, the numbers of observations and countries used in Table 4.3 differ from those in Table 4.2.

Table 4.7 Summary Statistics

	Mean	*Standard Deviation*	*Minimum Value*	*Maximum Value*	*Sample Size*
Log of GDP per Capita	8.84	1.43	5.60	11.59	1,219
Log of GDP per Capita without Government Spending	8.45	1.33	5.24	11.08	1,219
Domestic Competition Index	4.48	0.80	2.62	6.52	1,227
International Competition Index	4.47	0.69	2.80	6.10	1,159
Property Rights Index	4.14	0.80	2.70	6.20	1,227
Average Country Educational Attainment in Years	13.88	2.89	6.62	23.09	1,217
Log of the Country Working Age Population	4.88	1.58	1.10	9.55	1,224

Notes: Summary statistics for data used in the regressions. The unit of observation is a country's annual statistic between 2010 and 2019. The sample size for variables varies due to data availability. Depending on the regression specification and data availability, the maximum number of countries included in the regression models is 132.

Table 4.8 Effects of Domestic and International Competition and Property Rights on Country GDP per Capita: Controlling for Country and Year Effects

	GDP Per Capita			*GDP Per Capita without Government Spending*		
	(1)	*(2)*	*(3)*	*(4)*	*(5)*	*(6)*
Domestic Competition Index	0.114*** (0.030)			0.112*** (0.033)		
International Competition Index		0.024 (0.022)			0.044* (0.023)	
Property Rights Index			0.066*** (0.019)			0.073*** (0.025)
Observations	1,219	1,154	1,219	1,219	1,154	1,219
R-squared	0.521	0.489	0.508	0.456	0.431	0.449
Number of countries	132	123	132	132	123	132

*Notes: Estimated standard errors are in parentheses, below the point estimates. In Columns (1)–(3), the dependent variable is the annual 2010–2019 GDP per capita, and in Columns (4)–(6), the dependent variable is the annual 2010–2019 GDP per capita minus government spending per capita. Regressions include country- and year-fixed effects, educational attainment and the natural log of the country's population. The number of observations across specifications differs due to missing observations for some index values. Standard errors are clustered by country. Significance levels: * p<0.10, ** p<0.05, *** p<0.01.*

Table 4.9 Effects of Domestic and International Competition and Property Rights on Country GDP Per Capita: Controlling for Country and Year Effects, and Educational Attainment and Working Age Population

	GDP Per Capita			*GDP Per Capita without Government Spending*		
	(1)	*(2)*	*(3)*	*(4)*	*(5)*	*(6)*
Domestic Competition Index	0.109*** (0.029)			0.108*** (0.031)		
International Competition Index		0.023 (0.020)			0.044** (0.022)	
Property Rights Index			0.065*** (0.019)			0.070*** (0.023)
Observations	1,206	1,141	1,206	1,206	1,141	1,206

(*Continued*)

Table 4.9 (Continued)

	GDP Per Capita			*GDP Per Capita without Government Spending*		
	(1)	*(2)*	*(3)*	*(4)*	*(5)*	*(6)*
R-squared	0.559	0.530	0.549	0.524	0.504	0.517
Number of countries	130	121	130	130	121	130

*Notes: Estimated standard errors are in parentheses, below the point estimates. In Columns (1)–(3), the dependent variable is the annual 2010–2019 GDP per capita, and in Columns (4)–(6), the dependent variable is the annual 2010–2019 GDP per capita minus government spending per capita. Regressions include country- and year-fixed effects, educational attainment and the natural log of the country's working-age population. The number of observations across specifications differs due to missing observations for some index values or missing values for educational attainment, as well as the natural log of the country's working-age population. Standard errors are clustered by country. Significance levels: * $p<0.10$, ** $p<0.05$, *** $p<0.01$.*

We note that without government spending, a unit increase in IC leads to an increase in 4.4 per cent GDP per capita. A unit increase in DC score leads to an 11.2 per cent increase in GDP per capita. A unit increase in PR pillar score leads to an increase of 7.3 per cent GDP per capita.

Table 4.3 shows that the size and statistical significance of the estimates across specifications are similar to those in Table 4.2, including the estimates that adjust for government spending. All point estimates on the indices have a positive sign. As in Table 4.2, the estimates in Table 4.3 for the international competition index and the property rights index are larger when government spending is removed from GDP per capita.

The IC and PR scores have increased when government spending is removed, and the DC score impact has remained similar. It is still clear that the DC score is the biggest mover of the GDP per capita result.

This is certainly counterintuitive to policymaking where there has been a significant emphasis on international trade policy, and little focus on making domestic regulatory frameworks more pro-competitive. Policymakers should make efforts to improve all three pillar scores, as this can unleash significant wealth into their economies.

It is also important to note that these are effects that consider countries in isolation and do not account for their interactive effects on each other. We will look at other tools to develop these.

4.7 Do Developing Countries and Developed Countries Behave Differently?

We analysed whether differences in field effects of IC, DC and PR fields operated differently on developing countries as opposed to developed countries.

Table 4.10 Field Effects of IC, DC and PR Across All Countries

All countries					
Variable	*Obs*	*Mean*	*Std. Dev.*	*Min*	*Max*
gdppc	1,219	16253.4	20310.49	270.1373	108351.5
gdppc2	1,219	10057.31	12481.61	188.2932	64962.11
IC3	1,159	4.466437	0.6859771	2.8	6.2
DC	1,227	4.466539	0.8096363	2.548	6.524
PR	1,227	4.131377	0.8100118	2.2	6.2

Table 4.11 Field Effects of IC, DC and PR in the United Kingdom

United Kingdom					
Variable	*Obs*	*Mean*	*Std. Dev.*	*Min*	*Max*
gdppc	10	44600	1839.299	42310.75	47240.6
gdppc2	10	26275.15	2030.983	23385.57	28942.43
IC3	10	5.32	0.0421637	5.3	5.4
DC	10	5.7842	0.0563122	5.699	5.917
PR	10	5.67	0.1159502	5.4	5.8

One way of looking at this is to see how the United Kingdom behaves compared to other countries (see Tables 4.10 and 4.11 above).

We examined whether the results exhibit statistically different patterns for OECD countries (e.g. advanced, industrialised economies compared to developing or lower income economies). We found that the estimates for the OECD countries, as measured by the coefficients on the interaction terms, are not significantly different from the main estimates, and the conclusions from our baseline estimates apply to OECD countries.

4.8 Application of Physical Sciences to Economic Modelling

We have already discussed the application of an agency-based model which is drawn from econophysics. We now look at using probabilistic statistical mechanics techniques to understand voluntary exchanges (VEs) between buyers and sellers, and the impacts of field effects on them. These field effects arise from the impact of a country's policies in the areas of international trade, domestic competition and property rights protection to create environments in which buyers and sellers move and have their being. The statistical mechanics model is based on the assumption that interactions between buyers and sellers whose aggregate reflects wealth creation depend on the likelihood of interaction and the intensity of that interaction, which is in turn given by both a potential and kinetic term that can be analogised to potential and kinetic energy in a Hamiltonian operator. The VEs are analogised to particles that have particular probabilistic distributions based on a wavefunction. This lends itself to a model of wealth creation which draws on quantum formalism.

4.9 Why Might a Quantum Model Be Relevant to the Social Sciences?

Classical economics assumes that buyers and sellers operate like rational points in space and time, interacting when supply and demand curves meet (also at a specific point in space and time) in an optimised equilibrium. This assumes that those exchanges are deterministic and classical. The problem is that this equilibrium does not really exist in real life, and the exchanges are probabilistic not deterministic. As a result, the supply and demand curves of classical economics do not incorporate the real-world facts of innovation (wealth creating) and policy approaches that might be wealth reducing.

One of the problems with the equilibrium approach is that it underestimates the dynamic impact of distortions. The classical way of measuring this is to look at deadweight losses resulting from deviations from undistorted supply and demand curves.

Interestingly, all the different methods we have used to evaluate the impact of the three different fields illustrate similar differences between the fields. However, we believe that the quantum approach is likely to be the most accurate, as it alone factors in the second differential (rate of change of the rate of change of position in space of buyers and sellers) and thus is most likely to capture two elements that are missing from more classical economic analysis. The first is the dynamic effects of these interchanges economy-wide, and the second is the fact that buyers and sellers are created and annihilated based on the field effects on them (whereas classical economics assumes that they are conserved).

Economists have looked at the losses due to lack of competition based on deadweight losses. Harberger triangles and Tullock trapezia are graphical representations of the deadweight loss created by inefficiencies in markets, often due to monopolies, taxes or other distortions. They help visualise the economic costs of these inefficiencies.

4.9.1 Harberger Triangle

The Harberger triangle measures the deadweight loss from a change in price or quantity away from the competitive equilibrium.

The area of the triangle = 1/2 * base * height. The base is the change in quantity and the height is the difference between the competitive price and the actual price.

If a monopolist raises prices above the competitive level, the Harberger triangle represents the lost consumer and producer surplus due to the reduced quantity traded.

4.9.2 Tullock Trapezium

The Tullock trapezium measures the deadweight loss plus the rent-seeking costs associated with obtaining and maintaining a monopoly or other market distortion.

Area of the trapezium = 1/2 * (sum of parallel sides) * height. The parallel sides are the difference in output at the competitive and distorted prices. The height is the difference between the two prices.

If firms spend resources lobbying for government protection or engaging in anti-competitive practices, the Tullock trapezium captures both the lost surplus from the distorted market and the wasted resources spent on rent-seeking.

4.9.3 Key Differences Between the Two Approaches

Tullock trapezia explicitly include rent-seeking costs, while Harberger triangles do not. Consequently, Tullock trapezia generally show a larger deadweight loss than Harberger triangles because they account for a wider range of costs. While Tullock trapezia capture more of the losses from ACMDs, both methods underestimate the losses.

This problem has been analysed by Tullock, Posner and others in the 1970s. These scholars thought that the Harberger triangles underestimated the scale of efficiency losses caused by regulatory distortions that gave rise to monopoly. As a result, other methods of analysing these effects included the Tullock trapezium. Tullock and Posner both write important articles noting that Harberger triangles did not capture the full losses from distortive regulation, especially where that regulation tended to monopoly (i.e. where powerful incumbent secured regulation that gave them much-enhanced market power to the point of monopoly).[5] Posner has noted that there are losses that these models which are based on equilibrium approaches do not measure. The advantage of the probabilistic approach is that it is not based on a classical equilibrium and recognises the reality that for VE to take place in an undistorted fashion, the "system" must break out of equilibrium.[6] A dynamic system where buyers and sellers meet in VE is the *unstable* system, which always seeks to go back into a distorted equilibrium.

But both cases underestimate the actual wealth destruction that takes place because they are based on a fundamentally flawed normative framework, which is that the optimised economic system is an equilibrium. It is much more likely that the equilibrium is in fact highly distorted, giving rise to poverty and conflict, and that the optimised economic system is a world without ACMDs and that is a "far from equilibrium position". To analogise to the laws of thermodynamics, the state of highest entropy (the one that any economic system is strongly attracted to) is a highly distorted equilibrium, and that ordered state requires a significant amount of ongoing work to prevent the system from collapsing towards the distorted equilibrium point. This is consistent with one of the operating maxims of this book, which is that wealth can be created or destroyed but it is much harder to create than it is to destroy.

4.10 Application of Quantum Formalism

A more realistic explanation of what is happening is that two entities, call them x and y, are moving around in time and space, and when the conditions are right, they engage in VE where x gives a good or service, G to y and y gives money, M as a measurement of the value of G to x. M is merely a measurement of the value of G to y at that precise point in time and space. We can represent this by considering a VE occurring between the buyer and seller where the position and intensity of VE tell us what the wealth created by that VE occurs. Whether there is a VE is given by a probability distribution function (It is important to note that the probability distribution function describes the probability that VE occurs, not where buyers and sellers are located in some version of space and time). That probability density function applies to a "ground state" as well as a series of excited states that reflect factors outside of the IC, DC and PR pillars, which are the field strengths impacting the likelihood of buyers and sellers meeting in VE. These excited states reflect different probability distribution functions based on how these different forces (IC, DC and PR) are carried to buyers and sellers who are then more or less likely to engage in VE. These vectors which carry the forces of IC, DC and PR are differences in human capital, natural resources and the quality of institutions. We note that as field strengths increase, it may be possible to jump a particular country from one excited state to another or to shift it from the ground state, but that does not happen in a continuum. Small changes in force strength are unlikely to have any impact on how those forces are carried; only large changes can give rise to different probability distributions for different excited states.

As a result of this VE, wealth is created (given off like energy in a chemical reaction). As noted, these VEs between willing buyers and sellers are probabilistic in nature. There is a distribution of where they occur and a distribution of their intensities. Their intensities give us the wealth that is created from them. Since they are probabilistic, it is quite incorrect to model them on the basis that they are deterministic and predictable or that they are deterministic and stochastic. Classical economics therefore cannot help us here.

The classical economic approach has more in common with classical physics and laws of motion of particles. The approach advocated below has more in common with quantum mechanics where there is a probability distribution function for VEs occurring in some form of space.

4.11 Implications of Using Quantum Formalism

We are not saying that somehow actual buyers and sellers are subject to quantum mechanical laws in the sense in which quantum mechanics describes how subatomic particles behave. We are looking to see if quantum formalism and quantum concepts can help us better understand and create models that can more accurately explain how market distortions, especially ACMDs, can impact VE and how that affects the process of wealth creation. This can help us establish a normative framework to understand these concepts and develop equations that can be solved to show the impact of improvements in the three relevant dimensions or fields (international competition, domestic competition and property rights protection). We do this because the interaction between willing buyers and sellers in VE is a probabilistic process rather than a classically deterministic one. Given this, we know that applying classical economics cannot yield an accurate assessment of the wealth created when buyers and sellers meet in VE. Since classical economics cannot help, we must turn to probabilistic methodologies. This problem is one of the reasons classical economics' principles tend to underestimate consumer welfare losses from anti-competitive regulation and underestimate dynamic effects, even for dynamic stochastic general equilibrium models.

4.12 Application of Quantum Concepts

There is a significant amount of developing work by physicists applying quantum mechanical concepts to social science questions. The current classical economics approach is not dissimilar to classical Newtonian mechanics, in that it is deterministic and assumes that buyers and sellers are rational actors that interact with each other based on simple supply and demand curves, much like particles or points in space that interact with each other based on physical or electromechanical forces. A completely free market therefore enables buyers and sellers to find the point at which supply and demand curves meet to reveal the price of a given product at a particular time. This approach suggests that there is an optimised equilibrium point at which the system's efficiency is optimised.

Such an approach has historically not been strong in predicting the impacts of shifts in innovation or exogenous shocks to the economic system. A more dynamic approach starts from the assumption that systems do not necessarily rest in equilibria. Indeed, if there is an equilibrium position, it is towards the lower level of the three forces, and the ground state with regard to the three field vectors. The equilibrium position is then one characterised by poverty and fewer interactions. One has to work hard to increase the probability of VE and thus wealth creation.

Rather, dynamic assessments are more closely aligned with the principle that it is VE without distortion that maximises economic output and thus ln (GDP per capita) as a measure of economic value (i.e. productivity). Therefore, we assume that the IC (international competition or trade openness), DC (domestic competition) or PR (property rights) dimensions are represented by different forces, which interact with buyers and sellers (and even create them) in such a way that the intensity of their interactions creates wealth as a by-product (like a chemical reaction gives off energy as a by-product) (depending on how the field vectors carry these forces to buyers and sellers).

If we assume that IC, DC and PR are like interacting forces, we can postulate the three forces as the dimensions we have modelled in the SRB-γ model. The field is a proxy for the regulatory environment in country X viewed through the dimensions of IC, DC or PR. There may be other fields with other interactions on buyers and sellers, but we have assumed that these three fields are the most important based on the SRB-γ model's predictions. The SRB-γ model can thus be considered to be an experiment over a ten-year period from 2010 to 2019 for 118 countries that successfully tests the idea that these three fields have the strongest effects on potential buyers and sellers. We use the SRB-γ IC, PR and DC force scores as the potential term in an energy equation involving both a potential and kinetic term (see below).

4.12.1 Modelling the Forces and Field Vectors[7]

The starting point for constructing our quantum model is the quantum mechanical wave equation,

$$\left[\lambda \nabla_r^2 + V(\boldsymbol{r})\right]\Psi(\boldsymbol{r},t) = \mu \frac{\partial}{\partial t}\Psi(\boldsymbol{r},t)$$

where ∇_r^2 is the second-order partial differential Laplace operator in coordinates r. This is a partial differential equation that is second-order in $\boldsymbol{r}$ and first-order in t. When applied to atomic structure, the parameters λ and μ are chosen to give an equation involving energy, distance and time while satisfying dimensional requirements of the equation and take the form

$$\lambda = -\frac{\hbar^2}{2m_0} \; and \; \mu = -\frac{\hbar}{i}$$

where ħ is Planck's constant, h divided by 2π, in units of erg-seconds, m_0 is the electron mass in grams and *i* is the square root of minus one. This yields a Schrodinger wave equation for a hydrogen-like atom:

$$\left(-\frac{\hbar^2}{2m_0}\nabla_r^2 + V(\mathbf{r})\right)\Psi(r,\theta,\varphi,t) = -\frac{\hbar}{i}\frac{\partial}{\partial t}\Psi(r,\theta,\varphi,t)$$

The term in ∇_r^2 represents the kinetic energy of an electron and $V(\mathbf{r})$ represents the potential energy of an electron in the field of an atomic nucleus:

$$V(\mathbf{r}) = -\frac{Ze_0^2}{4\pi\varepsilon_0 r}$$

where Z is the magnitude of the nuclear charge, e_0 is the electron charge in coulombs, and ε_0 is the permittivity of free space in (farad/meter). The Schrodinger equation can be further reduced to a time-independent form through a separation of variables

$$\Psi(r,\theta,\varphi,t) = \psi(r,\theta,\varphi)\Phi(t)$$

where $\Phi(t)$ takes the form

$$\Phi(t) = e^{\frac{-iEt}{\hbar}}$$

and

$$-\frac{\hbar\partial}{i\partial t}\Phi(t) = E\Phi(t)$$

The wave equation, written in dimensional terms (distance in centimetres, time in seconds and energy in ergs), can be transformed into dimensionless form by defining dimensionless variables

$$\rho = r / a_0$$

$$\tau = t(\hbar/m_0 a_0^2)$$

$$\varepsilon = E / (\hbar^2 / m_0 a_0^2)$$

where a_0 is the Bohr orbit radius

$$a_0 = 4\pi\varepsilon_0[^2 / (e_0^2 m_0)$$

Multiplying the wave equation by (m_0 a_0^2 / $\hbar^2$), the Schrodinger equation becomes

$$\left(-\frac{1}{2}\nabla_A^2-\frac{Z}{\rho}\right)\Psi_k(\rho,\theta,\varphi,\tau)=\mathrm{i}\frac{\partial}{\partial\tau}\Psi_k(\rho,\theta,\varphi,\tau)=\varepsilon_k\Psi_k(\rho,\theta,\varphi,\tau)$$

The wavefunction Ψ_k represents the k-th eigenfunction of this equation. The lowest eigenfunctions take the form

$$\Psi_{100}(\rho,\theta,\varphi,\tau)=N_{100}e^{-\frac{Z\rho}{2}}e^{-i\varepsilon_{100}\tau}$$

$$\Psi_{200}(\rho,\theta,\varphi,\tau)=N_{200}\left(1-\frac{Z\rho}{2}\right)e^{-\frac{Z\rho}{2}}e^{-i\varepsilon_{200}\tau}$$

where N_k are corresponding normalisation constants and

$$\varepsilon_{100}=-\frac{Z^2}{2},\ \varepsilon_{200}=-\frac{Z^2}{8}$$

The wavefunctions are orthonormal

$$<\Psi_j\,|\,\Psi_k>=\iiint\rho^2\sin(\theta)d\rho\,d\theta\,d\varphi\Psi_j(\rho,\theta,\varphi,\tau)\Psi_k(\rho,\theta,\varphi,\tau)=\delta_{j,k}$$

4.12.2 The Quantum Problem of Interest

Returning now to the quantum mechanical wave equation as a starting point for building our quantum model,

$$\left[\lambda\nabla_r^2+V(r)\right]\Psi(r,t)=\mu\frac{\partial}{\partial t}\Psi(r,t)$$

The parameters λ and μ are chosen here to give an equation involving money, people and time, while satisfying dimensional requirements of the equation. They take the form

$$\lambda=-\frac{m^3}{p}\ and\ \mu=-\frac{Tm}{ip}$$

where m is a unit of money, p is a measure of population (the number of people), T is a measure of time and i is the square root of -1. The quantum wave equation is now

$$\left[-\frac{m^3}{p}\nabla_r^2+V(r)\right]\Psi(r,t)=-\frac{Tm}{ip}\frac{\partial}{\partial t}\Psi(r,t)$$

The potential term V is a mathematical representation of the interaction of the fields that affect VEs. The exact specification of V determines the nature of the solutions to the quantum wave equation. For now, we designate this as $V(F,r)$, where F denotes a combination of three dimensionless field strengths: IC, DC and PR. Here again, the wave equation can be further reduced to a time-independent form through a separation of variables

$$\Psi(r) = \psi(r)\Phi(t)$$

where $\Phi(t)$ takes the form

$$\Phi(t) = e^{\frac{-i\omega t}{Tm/p}}$$

and

$$-\frac{Tm}{ip}\frac{\partial}{\partial t}\Phi(t) = \omega\Phi(t)$$

The wave equation, written in dimensional terms (r in units of money m, t in units of time T and ω in units of m/p), can be transformed into dimensionless form by defining dimensionless variables

$$\rho = r / \mathrm{m}$$

$$\tau = t / T$$

$$\Omega = \omega / (\mathrm{m/p})$$

And multiplying the wave equation by p/m, it becomes

$$\left(-\nabla_A^2 + V(F,\rho)\Psi(\rho,\tau) = i\frac{\partial}{\partial\tau}\psi(\rho)\Phi(\tau) = \Omega\psi(\rho)\Phi(\tau)\right)$$

Equivalently, this wave equation can be written in terms of a Hamiltonian operator H

$$H\psi(\rho) = \Omega\psi(\rho)$$

where

$$H = \left[-\nabla_A^2 + V(F,\rho)\right]$$

and ψ is an eigenfunction of the operator H with the eigenvalue Ω. ψ represents the probabilistic distribution of VE for the potential field $V(F,\rho)$.

4.11.3 Modelling the Forces and Field Vectors

H is the Hamiltonian operator which describes the interaction effect between the field F and the entity in the field ψ . The relevant fields F are the IC, DC and PR fields. Here, the eigenvalue Ω is a "wealth creation" quantity corresponding to wealth that is created by a given VE governed by a given Hamiltonian, H (field) which will differ among the three fields, and within each of those fields between countries.

$$\text{H}(\text{IC, DC, PR})\psi = (\text{IC, DC, PR})\psi$$

The relevant SRB-γ equations are as follows:

Equation DC: $$ln(y_t) = \beta_{D0} + \boldsymbol{\beta}_{D1} Domestic\,Competition_{it} + \beta_{D2} Expected\,Years\,of\,Schooling_{it} + \beta_{D3} lpop_{it} + \beta_{D4} Expenditure\,of\,GDP_{it} + \nu_t + \lambda_i + \epsilon_{it}$$

Equation PR: $$ln(y_t) = \beta_{D0} + \boldsymbol{\beta}_{D1} Domestic\,Competition_{it} + \beta_{D2} Expected\,Years\,of\,Schooling_{it} + \beta_{D3} lpop_{it} + \beta_{D4} Expenditure\,of\,GDP_{it} + \nu_t + \lambda_i + \epsilon_{it}$$

Equation IC: $$ln(y_t) = \beta_{D0} + \boldsymbol{\beta}_{D1} Domestic\,Competition_{it} + \beta_{D2} Expected\,Years\,of\,Schooling_{it} + \beta_{D3} lpop_{it} + \beta_{D4} Expenditure\,of\,GDP_{it} + \nu_t + \lambda_i + \epsilon_{it}$$

We use the IC, PR and DC pillar scores and we approximate these pillar scores to three distinct forces whose strength impacts where the VE can be found in the relevant space. The stronger the forces, the more likely VE will be found close to the y-axis of the probabilistic distribution of potential VEs. The closer the VE is likely to be at the y-axis, the more powerful the wealth creating impact of the VE.

We now have an approximation for a Hamiltonian for each of the fields. This Hamiltonian will differ for a specific country and a specific field based on the DC, IC and PR parameters, which are derived from the SRB-γ model regressions and statistical weightings. We know these parameters from the 2010–2019 panel data of 118 countries constitute a robust and significant correlation (see SRB-γ model analysis in Chapter X).

4.12.4 Interpretation of the Wave Equation

The kinetic term of the Hamiltonian will be applied to a wave function, which describes the probability distribution function of VEs. In quantum mechanics, the wavefunction is the probabilistic distribution of particles with respect to their position (or angular momentum) in space across dimensions of x, y and z. By analogy, here, the wavefunction is the probabilistic distribution of VEs between buyers and sellers at any point in country X or between country X and country Y as described by the Hamiltonian. Hence, $\psi(f)$ is a linear combination of all solutions ψ to the equation. That is, ψ consists of all possible buyers' and sellers' VEs that will contribute to $\boldsymbol{\Omega}$.

The interaction between the forces and the fields in which they are embedded for a given country and the wave function have different effects on the VEs occurring in the fields represented. The IC, DC and PR scores reflect forces which operate on buyers and sellers making VE more or less likely and impacting the intensity of it, and thus the wealth created as a result.

These forces are communicated to the probability density function of VEs through three fields: institutional strength, natural resources and human capital. These fields represent different configurations that countries are in. The wavefunction for these different configurations is approximated by a set of ground or excited states that the country may be in, depending on how these fields attenuate the forces that impact the probability of VE.

The application of the three forces, IC, DC and PR, to the probabilistic distribution of VEs between buyers and sellers generates more and more intense VEs in these states, which are reflected by the potential and kinetic terms. Changing the IC, DC or PR forces scores leads to a new and/or stronger VE, which is different in terms of position and intensity. We can apply changes to the IC, DC and PR forces to assess how the "energy" or "wealth creation" numbers are affected. Each country has a ground and series of excited states based on the field vectors that carry the forces into the interactions. Where they are in those configurations depends on the three field vectors, institutions, human capital and natural resources. We have evaluated for the United Kingdom, the United States and China for these configurations. It is possible that strong enough forces can lead countries to move into different configurations, although this requires large changes in force.

We can derive this wealth creation from equations of motion with kinetic and potential energy terms. This is akin to VEs with different levels of efficiency, which leads to greater or lesser amounts of wealth creation released when the VEs take place. These excitations represent different states derived from specific improvements in the IC, PR and DC scores from the SRB-γ model equations, which are themselves derived from physically observable reality over 118 countries and ten years' panel data. In this way, we are using physically observable information to set out the Hamiltonian.

By measuring the impact of the IC, DC and PR forces on the VE wavefunctions, we can compute the impact of the excitation on these wavefunctions and the consequent impact on VE, including their creation and annihilation (this being a proxy for entrepreneurialism/creative destruction). Unlike energy or angular momentum, in our economic universe, wealth can be created or destroyed.

4.12.5 Specification of the Potentials and Wavefunctions

The Hamiltonian, H , is written in terms of a solvable zeroth-order Hamiltonian, H_0 , and a first-order Hamiltonian, H_1 , as follows:

$$H = H_0 + H_1 \text{ and } V = V_0 + V_1$$

$$H_0(k) = \sum_k \left[-\nabla_A^2 + V_0(F,\rho)\right]_k \, and \, H_0(k)\psi_k = \Omega_k \psi_k$$

where H_0 includes kinetic and potential interaction terms and the summation index, *k,* runs over the IC, DC and PR spaces. The wavefunctions, ψ_k, are taken from the set of eigenfunctions of the zeroth-order dimensionless Hamiltonian. The first-order Hamiltonian involves further interactions between the fields,

$$H_1 = V_1(F,\rho)$$

The zeroth-order and first-order corrections to Ω are as follows:

$$\Omega = \Omega_0 + \Omega_1 \text{ and } \Omega_0 = \sum_k \Omega_0(k) \text{ and } \Omega_1 = \sum_{i<j} \int \psi_i H_1 \psi_j$$

and the wavefunctions, ψ, are expanded as a linear combination of basis functions, φ, with linear coefficients, $b_{i,j}$:

$$\psi = \Sigma_{i<j} b_{i,j} \, \varphi(i)\varphi(j)$$

A number of different potentials can be used. One of these choices is a reciprocal ρ potential leading to an exponential wavefunction. For instance,

$$V(Z,\rho) = -\frac{Z}{\rho^n(\rho \pm c)}$$

where n ≤ 1 and c is an arbitrary constant. For the dimensionless quantum wave equation described earlier, n = 0 and c = 0 gives the potential

$$V(Z,\rho) = -\frac{Z}{\rho}$$

The corresponding wavefunctions represent the probabilistic distribution of the three fields. In this case, the wavefunctions, ψ , are given by exp(-Zρ) for the ground states or $\exp(-Z\rho/2)(1 - Z\rho/2)$ for an excited state, where Z corresponds to the Z_{IC}, Z_{DC} or Z_{PR} , interaction strength. The first wavefunction has the form of the ground state eigenfunction of the zero-order

Hamiltonian. The second wavefunction has the form of the first excited state eigenfunction of the zero-order Hamiltonian.

We then apply the quantum wave equation to generate the ground and first excited states we discussed. The quantum wave equation for this system involves a Hamiltonian, $H = H_0 + H_1$, where H_0 has kinetic and potential energy terms and H_1 has repulsive interaction terms:

$$H_0 = \sum_k \left(-\frac{1}{2}\nabla_k^2 - \frac{Z_k}{\left(\rho_k^{n_k} - C_k\right)} \right) and\, H_1 = +\sum_{i,j} \frac{Z_i Z_j}{\rho_{ij}}$$

Here, the summation over k corresponds to the three forces, IC, DC and PR. The summation over i,j corresponds to interaction between the forces two at a time. Calculation of $\Omega = \int \psi | H | \psi$ with $\int \psi | \psi = 1$ is then straightforward.

1. We assume that the potential term, which would normally be a potential energy term, is described as a potential wealth creation term (GDP per capita is a proxy for wealth creation). $\mathrm{PWC}(Z) = Z/\left(\rho^{n} + C\right)$ where Z is the strength of the field interaction. If $n = 1$ and $C = 0$, then this interaction is analogous to an electrostatic attraction.
2. We assume that the PR term has a "stronger" field effect. This is because PR is the fundamental basis for the DC and IC terms. Without PR, there is nothing for firms to compete with. We take $\mathrm{PWC}\ (\mathrm{PR}) = Z_{PR}/\rho$ where Z_{PR} is the strength of the PR interaction. In this case, there is a wavefunction corresponding to the PR field that is an eigenfunction of the PR Hamiltonian.
3. DC and IC are "weaker" fields (for instance, gravity compared with the electrostatic force). Between IC and DC, IC is more dominant where ρ is large; DC is more dominant as ρ comes down (cf. strong and weak nuclear forces).
4. IC, DC and PR are the fundamental forces that drive wealth creation. There may be other forces, we do not discount that, but their effects are minimal compared to these three.
5. $\mathrm{PWC}(\mathrm{IC}) = -Z_{IC}/\ (\rho^{u} + C_{IC})$ where Z_{IC} is the strength of the IC interaction. The constant C_{IC} is an arbitrary parameter to be determined. If C_{IC} is zero, and if $u = 2$, then this potential term would be analogous to a gravitational attraction. However, μ could take on the value 1, such that the IC wavefunction could be an eigenvalue of its Hamiltonian equation. Alternatively, u can be assigned an arbitrary value that is determined to be most suitable for the IC field.
6. $\mathrm{PWC}\ (\mathrm{DC}) = -Z_{DC}/\ \left(\rho^{v} + C_{DC}\right)$ where Z_{DC} is the strength of the DC interaction. Here again, there is a similar flexibility in assigning a value to v and C_{DC}.

Hamiltonian with Gaussian Eigenfunction

Another possibility for the potential field and corresponding wave functions is a Gaussian distribution model. The potential takes the form

$$V(F,\rho)=\mathcal{V}\left(F_x\rho_x,F_y\rho_y,F_z\rho_z\right)$$

We now define the variables: $x=\rho_x$, $y=\rho_y$ and $z=\rho_z$. The wavefunction becomes

$$\psi(\alpha,n,x)=N_n(\alpha)e^{-\alpha x^2/2}\mathrm{H}_n\left(\sqrt{\alpha}x\right)$$

where $N_n(\alpha)$ is a normalisation constant

$$N_n(\alpha)=\left[\frac{1}{2^n n!}\sqrt{\frac{\alpha}{\pi}}\right]^{\frac{1}{2}}$$

and H_n is the nth-order Hermite polynomial. The wavefunction is normalised,

$$\int_{-\infty}^{\infty}\psi(\alpha,n,x)\psi(\alpha,n,x)dx=1$$

We define the field strengths: $\mathrm{A}=\mathrm{IC}$, $\mathrm{B}=\mathrm{DC}$, $\mathrm{C}=\mathrm{PR}$ in the corresponding spaces x, y, z and the corresponding states i, j, k. The total wavefunction is then defined as $\Psi(A,i,x;B,j,y;C,k,z)$

$$=\psi(\sqrt{A(A+B+C)},i,x)\,\psi(\sqrt{B(A+B+C)},j,y)$$
$$\psi(\sqrt{C(A+B+C)},k,z)$$

The total wavefunction is normalised,

$$\iint\int_{-\infty}^{\infty}\Psi(A,i,x;B,j,y;C,k,z)\Psi(A,i,x;B,j,y;C,k,z)\,dxdydz=1$$

The Hamiltonian, including kinetic, ∇^2, and potential, $V(F,\rho)$, terms is

$$H=(-\nabla_x^{\ 2}-\nabla_y^{\ 2}-\nabla_z^{\ 2})+A^2x^2+B^2y^2+C^2z^2)$$
$$+(AB)(x-y)^2+(AC)(x-z)^2+(BC)(y-z)^2$$

The zeroth-order and first-order perturbative Hamiltonians are

$$H_0=(-\nabla_x^{\ 2}-\nabla_y^{\ 2}-\nabla_z^{\ 2})+A(A+B+C)x^2$$
$$+B(A+B+C)y^2+C(A+B+C)z^2$$

$$H_1=-2ABxy-2ACxz-2BCyz$$

The perturbative wavefunction, $\Psi(A,i,x;B,j,y;C,k,z)$, is an eigenfunction of the zeroth-order Hamiltonian

$$H_0\Psi = \Omega_0\Psi$$

where

$$\Omega_0 = \left[(2i+1)\sqrt{A} + (2j+1)\sqrt{B} + (2k+1)\sqrt{C}\right]\sqrt{A+B+C}$$

and the expectation value of the Hamiltonian through first-order with respect to the total wavefunction is

$$\iint \int_{-\infty}^{\infty} \Psi\left|H_0 + H_1\right|\Psi \, dx\, dy\, dz = \Omega_1$$

4.12.7 Application of Ground and Excited States to Hamiltonian Calculations

We have made calculations as to the likely configurations of three key countries, the United States, the United Kingdom and China, and looked at the impact on the Hamiltonians of these different configurations. The matrices for each of these countries and respective configurations from which we can construct estimates of excited states are set out below.

Excited states reflect how IC, DC and PR forces are communicated to VE probability through the strength of institutions (I), human capital (HC) and natural resources (NR). In the econometric model, we control for these in the equations that specify the model. Here, we use them as vectors that carry forces to the probability density function for VEs.

Each country may be in the ground state configuration or in a potential excited state. These excited states apply to IC, DC and PR individually and in combination. This gives rise to potentially seven excited states. These include

E1: IC (e), DC, PR,
E2: IC, DC (e), PR
E3: IC, DC, PR (e)
E4: IC (e), DC (e), PR
E5: IC (e), DC. PR (e)
E6: IC, DC (e), PR (e)
E7: IC (e), DC (e), PR (e)

We assess the impact of the three fields (I, HC and NR) on the forces (IC, DC and PR). This reflects the reality that improvements in forces in countries that are poor performers on the fields will suffer an attenuation of the force effects on the probability of VE. Each country is in a specific configuration.

Country X may be in configuration E4, for example, with specific IC, DC and PR force strengths. Small increases in IC, DC and PR force strengths are unlikely to have an impact on the configuration. But one can imagine that a big increase in IC, DC and/or PR scores could cause a country to jump into a different excited state. Country X with a big increase in IC, DC or PR, for example, could lead to a jump from E4 to E5 or higher. This will be reflected in a much bigger increase in GDP per capita because of the transition than if the country remained in the E4 excited state. It is also not automatic that the wealth created from force strength increases is automatically higher with each of the excited states. It is possible that different excited states operate differently. It is easy to see that DC changes are likely to have a bigger impact on the strength of institutions, and human capital, thus making a jump to DC(e) much more likely. If IC improves but DC decreases or stays the same, it is possible that the gatekeepers of the economy (see Chapters 1 and 2 for the privatisations in the former Soviet Union, for example) will be strengthened, it may be that I and HC field effects will actually decrease. We saw similar things in the transitions in the 1990s in the former Soviet Union and Latin America, which we discussed in Chapters 1 and 2, where opening up to trade without improving conditions of competition inside the border led to a building up of oligarchic power. This in turn damaged fragile institutions which were subject to political forces. Had trade opening been accompanied by improving domestic competition, institution quality would have increased, as those same fragile institutions would have been strengthened by economic forces.

The assessments for the United Kingdom, China and the United States are as follows.

United Kingdom Field Effects

We assign a score of between 1 and 5 to the NR, HC and I rating for each country. We have assessed these effects in the following matrix (Table 4.12):

Table 4.12 The UK Field Effects

DC	*IC*	*PR*	
1	1	1	NR
4	4	5	HC
4	4	3	I

Note the 1 field scores for NR are based on the available and usable natural resources. The United Kingdom currently bans coal, North Sea oil and gas, fracking and has a very delayed nuclear capability. These could change, and if they do, given the fact that the United Kingdom has significant natural resources (albeit unexploited), these could change to 4s or even 5s.

DC (3), IC (3), PR (3)

United States Field Score

We have assumed that the United States will fully exploit its natural resources for the purposes of the matrix given herein (Table 4.13):.

Table 4.13 The US Field Score

DC	*IC*	*PR*	
5	5	5	NR
5	4	5	HC
5	4	4	I

Table 4.14 China Field Score

DC	*IC*	*PR*	
4	4	4	NR
2	2	1	HC
1	1	1	I

DC (5), IC (4), PR (5). We can assume that the United States is in the highest excited state.

China Field Score (Table 4.14)

Table 4.15 Quantum Model Parameters

Quantum Model Parameters						
	IC	*DC*	*PR*	*Excited State Field Scores*		
UK	4.700	5.917	5.400	IC(3)	DC(3)	PR(3)
US	5.100	5.895	5.600	IC(4)	DC(5)	PR(4)
China	5.600	4.421	4.300	IC(2)	DC(2)	PR(2)

DC (2), IC (2), PR (2).

These excited states can be used to solve the one-country problem.

By measuring the impact of the IC, DC and PR forces on the VE wavefunctions, we can compute the impact of the excitation on the wavefunctions, Ψ, and the consequent impact on VE and Ω, including their creation and annihilation (this being a proxy for entrepreneurialism/creative destruction). The following table (Table 4.15) gives a preliminary example showing the effect of increases of magnitude Δ, where $\Delta = 0.1$, 0.5 and 1.0 in various combinations of the field strengths IC, DC and PR on Ω for the United Kingdom, the United States and China using the average excited state field effect scores given earlier.

Percentage increase in Q for changes of A in field strengths IC, DC and PR (with A = 0.1) is given in Table 4.16.

Table 4.16 Percentage Increase Ω for Changes of Δ in Field Strengths IC, DC and PR (with $\Delta = 0.1$)

	(IC)+Δ	*(DC)+Δ*	*(PR)+Δ*	*(IC,DC)+Δ*	*(IC,PR)+A*	*(DC,PR)+Δ*	*(IC,DC,PR)+Δ*
UK	0.64%	0.61%	0.62%	1.25%	1.27%	1.23%	1.88%
US	0.59%	0.64%	0.57%	1.23%	1.16%	1.22%	1.80%
China	0.67%	0.71%	0.72%	1.38%	1.39%	1.43%	2.10%

Percentage increase in Q for changes of A in field strengths IC, DC and PR (with A = 0.5) is given in Table 4.17.

Table 4.17 Percentage Increase Ω for Changes of Δ in Field Strengths IC, DC, PR (with $\Delta = 0.5$)

	(IC)+Δ	*(DC)+Δ*	*(PR)+Δ*	*(IC,DC)+Δ*	*(IC,PR)+Δ*	*(DC,PR)+Δ*	*(IC,DC,PR)+Δ*
UK	3.20%	3.03%	3.09%	6.25%	6.31%	6.14%	9.39%
US	2.91%	3.19%	2.85%	6.13%	5.78%	6.07%	9.02%
China	3.34%	3.53%	3.55%	6.90%	6.92%	7.12%	10.51%

Percentage increase in Q for changes of A in field strengths IC, DC and PR (with A = 1.0) is given in Table 4.18.

Table 4.18 Percentage Increase Ω for Changes of Δ in Field Strengths IC, DC, PR (with $\Delta = 1.0$)

	ss	*(DC)+Δ*	*(PR)+Δ*	*(IC,DC)+Δ*	*(IC,PR)+Δ*	*(DC,PR)+Δ*	*(IC,DC,PR)+Δ*
UK	6.34%	6.01%	6.14%	12.45%	12.58%	12.24%	18.77%
US	5.78%	6.35%	5.66%	12.22%	11.51%	12.10%	18.04%
China	6.64%	7.00%	7.05%	13.74%	13.79%	14.17%	21.02%

Preliminary results for China, the United States and the United Kingdom suggest that a 1.0 increase in the IC, DC and PR scores could yield around 18–20 per cent GDP per capita increase. This is roughly in accord with the SRB-γ model.

We will be producing new estimates in the future. We will also be looking at how countries affect each other's growth. We will also be developing more robust ways of assigning configurations of excited states to countries.

4.12.8 Evolution of Model to Multi-Country Problem

The above shows how we intend to solve the one-country problem. What happens when we introduce multi-country problems, ultimately introducing all 118 countries in our model? We are particularly interested in the impact of the different force score changes on other countries. This is important because the

United States is currently thinking about how to calculate the impact of changing force effects on their pillar scores and therefore on their GDP per capita.

One way of solving our one-country problem and applying it to multi-country problems is to use a Gaussian mixture model (GMM). Future work on this area will consider the application of GMMs to this problem.

4.12.9 Gaussian Mixture Model

The Gaussian mixture model (GMM) is a probabilistic model that assumes that the data points come from a limited set of Gaussian distributions with uncertain variables. The mean and covariance matrix characterises each individual Gaussian distribution.

As an extension of the k-means clustering technique, a GMM takes into account the data's covariance structure and the likelihood of each point being derived from each Gaussian distribution.

GMM Algorithm

Clustering algorithms like the GMM in machine learning are used to organise data by identifying commonalities and distinguishing them from one another. It may be used to classify consumers into subgroups defined by factors like demographics and buying habits.

Each data point is given a chance of belonging to each cluster, making it a soft GMM clustering technique. This provides more leeway and may accommodate scenarios when data points do not naturally fall into one cluster.

The GMM is trained using the EM algorithm, an iterative approach for determining the most likely estimations of the mixture Gaussian distribution parameters. The EM method first makes rough guesses at the parameters, and then repeatedly improves those guesses until convergence is reached.

How the GMM algorithm works:

- **Initialise phase:** Gaussian distributions' parameters should be initialised (means, covariances and mixing coefficients).
- **Expectation phase:** Determine the likelihood that each data point was created using each of the Gaussian distributions.
- **Maximisation phase:** Apply the probabilities found in the expectation step to re-estimate the Gaussian distribution parameters.
- **Final phase**: To achieve convergence of the parameters, repeat steps 2 and 3.

4.13 Summary of Models

We note some key elements of all of the models above. First, the scale of impact of changing the IC, DC and PR scores is much larger than previously thought. Second, all the models, including the probabilistic one, come up with very similar orders of magnitude for the impact of the three fields with respect to each other. Typically, a unit increase in pillar scores has an impact of 10–25 per cent in terms of GDP per capita change. This is significant enough to warrant further study and for policymakers to prioritise a reduction of ACMDs.

The Agent-Based Model (ABM) shows that internal measures of the same type as border measures impose a loss that is typically three times greater. This is similar to the difference between IC and DC field effects. When all these different models tell us similar things, policymakers can be confident that changes of policy that improve DC especially are particularly powerful.

The quantum model is still in development but has many attractions. It is the only model that is probabilistic in a way that human interactions and the likelihood of VE are probabilistic. It can help us solve the one-country model and we can apply other probabilistic techniques to illustrate how one-country effects can change the likelihood and intensity of VE in other countries.

Notes

1 The work on the SRB-γ model refinements was done in collaboration with the Centre for Economics and Business Research, and with Professor Tom Stratmann, George Mason University and Christine McDaniel, Mercatus Center at George Mason University

2 Singham, Shanker A., Rangan, U. Srinivasa, and Bradley, Robert F. (2016, September). *Introduction to Anti-Competitive Market Distortions and the Distortions Index*. Legatum Institute, available at: LIIntro-to-ACMDDistortionsIndex.pdf. We also refer to work done by the Centre for Business Research on the development of the SRB model; See also Anticompetitive Market Distortions: Causes, Consequences and Corrections, for OECD-World Bank Conference, May 2015, Singham, Rangan, and Bradley, available at: Anticompetitive Market Distortions: Causes, Consequences, and Corrections - Draft.

3 The SRB- γ results section was contributed by our collaborators on this work, Christine McDaniel and Tom Stratmann, of the Mercatus Centre, and George Mason University respectively.

4 The Growth Commission, *The Growth Budget 2023* (November 2023), https://assets-global.website-files.com/646a30e30500c46bb82472c0/65534d5cc6f65dfbfcca6752_FINAL%20Growth%20Budget%202023%20DIGITAL%20SPREAD%20(1).pdf.

5 See Posner, Richard A. (1975). The Social Costs of Monopoly and Regulation. *Journal of Political Economy* 83(4), 807–827; See also Tullock, Gordon. (1967, June). The Welfare Costs of Tariffs, Monopolies, and Theft. *Western Economic Journal* 5(3), 224–232.

6 For an analysis of dynamic systems out of equilibrium, see Prigogine, Ilya, and Stengers, Isabelle. (2017). *Order Out of Chaos: Man's New Dialogue with Nature*. Verso Books.

7 This work was developed though a collaboration between the author and David Silver, former Director of the Johns Hopkins Applied Physics Laboratory.

5 Review of Global Growth Trajectory if ACMDs had been properly dealt with

5.1 What If ACMDs Had Been Dealt with When Liberalisation Occurred in the 1990s?

While we cannot do anything to change the past, it is an interesting thought experiment to look at how events may have worked out differently if anti-competitive market distortions (ACMDs) had been better managed in the 1990s in the manner we suggest in this monograph. The failure to deal properly with ACMDs behind the border led to the opening of markets at the border, but did not do anything to improve conditions of competition inside the border. Prices that consumers take in markets depend on the conditions of competition in those markets, and for consumers to see the benefits in lower prices of products because of more import competition, that competition must flow through the border into the import market itself. Where that does not occur, then the price benefits to consumers can be captured and GDP per capita growth takes place inside the import market. Note that in our ACMD model domestic regulatory reform, the domestic competition field has the biggest effect (roughly double the effect of conventional border measures). Therefore, if we are not changing the domestic competition field, but instead maintaining a low score, there will be limited gains from trade liberalisation. While the latest version of the SRB model looks at each field separately, previous models attempt to understand the interaction effects of the different fields, and there is some initial evidence that countries that liberalised trade while keeping domestic competition field unchanged experienced GDP per capita losses.

We look at some specific case studies.

5.1.1. China and the Multi-Fibre Agreement

When China acceded to the WTO in 2001, its textile firms were very large state-owned enterprises. According to CEIC data, the employment data for the textile industry reached an all-time high of 56 per cent[1] in 2008. The WTO's MFA had a specific quota for developed country markets that served to protect

DOI: 10.4324/9781003570608-5

textile producers from smaller developing countries. The MFA expired in 2005 and so the impacts of Chinese ACMDs in the textile sector were immediately felt. In fact, they resulted in wiping out almost all the small Central American textile producers. The US feels the effect of this action today with waves of migration from poor Central Americans seeking to leave their countries and the lack of opportunity there.[2]

If a mechanism to deal with ACMDs existed at this time, producers in affected countries could have sued to protect their existing quotas on the basis that loss of the quota would lead to damage based on the impact of China ACMDs. These industries would then have had time to transition, become more efficient and go up the value chain. The damage to Central American economies could have been averted.

Such a mechanism could look like this. In addition to a mechanism where a producer could apply for a tariff where they were able to prove a market distortion, and prove anti-competitive effect, causation and damage, so too could a producer in country C seek an extension of a quota or preference in country A on the basis that exporters from Country B into Country A are imposing ACMDs on the market of country B, giving exporters of country B an unfair cost advantage derived not from efficiency, but rather from the ACMD itself. Had such a process been available to Central American exporters, they would have been able to transition at a reasonable pace as opposed to losing access to the US market overnight. But this would have required an understanding of the ACMDs in the textile sector in China and its effects not just on producers in export markets, but also on third-country markets.

5.1.2 China Steel Distortions

Perhaps the area where Chinese market distortions have had the most well-studied impact is in the steel sector. This has had a profound impact on steel producers in the United States, the European Union and the United Kingdom. Steel mills have been shuttered in Port Talbot, Redcar in the UK. In the United States, some 48,000 steel jobs have been lost since 2000. China became a WTO member in 2001 and then had access to global markets. However, its steel sector was highly subsidised and benefited from a range of ACMDs (such as free water, free energy, free land and free credit – all vital pre-requisites for the production of steel). These distortions had a significant impact on G7 steel producers (See Figure 5.1 below). It is important to point out that China was not the only distorter, although its distortions are of a different nature from those in (and perhaps of different order of magnitude and length of time), for example, Japan or Korea. Government subsidies have frequently been used to prop up the steel industry in many countries. This is perhaps one of the reasons that steel exports from Japan and Korea have not declined after China's WTO accession (in other words, there was limited or no substitution of Japanese

	2000	2001	2002	2003	2004	2005	2006	2007	2008	2009	2011	2012	2013	2014	2015	2016
Japan	28.5	29.5	35.2	33.7	34.8	32	34.6	35.6	36.9	33.3	40.7	41.5	42.5	41.3	40.8	40.5
Russia	27.5	25.6	27.7	32.3	30.4	30.9	31.5	29.4	28.4	27.6	24.7	26.7	23.6	27	29.7	31.2
Germany	24.5	23.9	24.7	24.7	28.2	26	29.2	29.9	28.6	20.8	26.4	26	24.3	24.8	25.1	25.1
China	10.8	7.5	6.6	8.5	20.1	27.4	51.7	66.4	58.3	24	47.9	54.8	61.5	92.9	111.6	108.1
United States	6.2	5.7	5.5	7.5	7.3	9.4	9.6	9.8	12	9.2	13.3	13.6	12.5	12	10	9.2
Ukraine	22.3	24.4	25.9	26.6	28.2	27.3	30.6	30.3	28.6	24	26	24.1	24.7	21.5	17.7	18.2
Canada	5.1	4.6	5.6	5.5	5.4	6	6.1	6.8	7.4	4.9	6.4	6.2		6.2	6	5.8
United Kingdom	7.8	6.9	6.6	7.3	7.8	8.7	8.5	9.5	8.9	6.3	6	6.4	8.4	8.6	7.3	
France	17.5	16.9	17.6	17.5	18.7	17.6	18.8	18.2	17.1	12	14.2	14.6	14.2	14.9	14	13.7
South Korea	13.9	14	12.9	14.1	15	16.1	18	18.3	19.7	20.2	28.9	30.2	28.9	31.9	31.2	30.6

Figure 5.1 Steel Exporters and Their Share (2000–2016)[3]

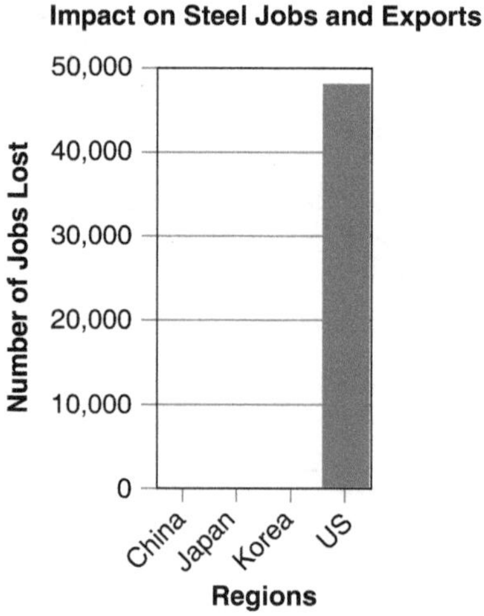

Figure 5.2 Impact on Steel Jobs and Overall Exports

or Korean steel by China products). Indeed, the impact of China ACMDs, coupled with more traditional subsidies in Japan and Korea, merely eroded the United States' and United Kingdom's steel industry markets while not especially impacting Japanese and Korean steel producers.

We can see from Figure 5.2 that the job loss in this sector has been heavily concentrated in the United States, leading to significant political economy challenges for the US government.

Driven by this political reality, attempts to resolve the issue of market distortions are probably most advanced when it comes to trade in steel. There has been a long history of trying to resolve the issue of distortions in the steel sector.

5.1.3 History of Steel Sector's Attempts to Solve Distortions

1. **Public Body Cases in WTO**:

   - The World Trade Organization (WTO) has been a primary forum for addressing trade distortions in the steel sector. Over the years, several member countries have brought cases against others, alleging that they provided unfair subsidies to their domestic steel industries. These subsidies, often provided by "public bodies" (government entities), were seen as distorting global steel markets.
   - For instance, the United States and the European Union have frequently raised concerns about China's state-owned enterprises providing

subsidies to its steel industry, leading to overcapacity and steel dumping in global markets. These concerns led to several disputes at the WTO, where member countries sought remedies against such practices.

Reference

1. **EU–US Steel Agreements**:
   - The European Union and the United States have a long history of negotiations and agreements concerning the steel sector. These agreements have often addressed trade distortions, such as dumping and subsidies.

1. Both sides have previously imposed tariffs and counter-tariffs on steel imports. However, through negotiations, they have often reached agreements to reduce or eliminate these tariffs, ensuring a level playing field for steel producers on both sides of the Atlantic.

Trilateral Group on Market Distortions:

- Recognising the global nature of steel market distortions, major steel-producing countries, including the United States, the European Union and Japan, formed a trilateral group to address these issues.
- This group aimed to tackle global overcapacity, unfair subsidies and other market-distorting practices in the steel sector. The trilateral group sought to promote fair trade practices and ensure a sustainable global steel industry through dialogue and cooperation.[4]

These efforts represent a continuous attempt by major steel-producing countries to address the challenges posed by market distortions in the steel sector. Over the years, these countries have sought to ensure a fair and competitive global steel market through negotiations, disputes and cooperative mechanisms. Regrettably, the trilateral group has seen little progress on this issue.

Indeed, none of these has really addressed the core problem, which is the impact on market competition of the various government practices in the sector.

5.2 The Rise of Oligarchic Power in the Former Soviet Bloc, Asia and Latin America

Failure to focus on market conditions and, specifically, whether they are pro-competitive meant that when liberalisation came to the countries of the former Soviet Union post-transition, or the Latin American markets after decades of import substitution economics, or India post the reforms initiated in 1991, it was not accompanied by competition on the merits inside the border. This meant that the gains of liberalisation (in increased competition and lower prices) were captured by the gatekeepers of the economy, but few, if any, of those gains flowed to consumers. This was especially true of the wave of privatisation, which tended to take a public monopoly with regulation and replace it with a private monopoly without regulation.[5] Once oligarchic or monopoly power is established, it is notoriously difficult to lessen. My book on privatisation shows this power at work in a number of sectors, especially telecommunications in Mexico.[6]

Had concrete work on distortions accompanied the liberalisation that took place in the 1990s, the oligarchic, vested interests would not have been able to so easily to ensure that the domestic regulatory landscape protected their position, preserving and exacerbating an anti-competitive landscape that destroys wealth out of the economy. Global GDP per capita would have increased in accordance with pre-2000s trends at least, but, one would anticipate, could have risen by much more.

The graph herein shows the increase in global GDP per capita between 1980 and 2016. We focus in particular on the period 1996 and 2016. We assume that gains in the IC pillar score correlate to improvements in international trade for all countries. Without changing IC pillar scores, we next assume that there were no changes of significance to the DC pillar scores. We assume that PR pillar scores did improve with, for example, developments like the TRIPS agreement, which led to better protection of intellectual property rights. We know that the SRB-γ model calculates GDP per capita gains and there is no difference between these impacts whether we are talking about OECD countries or non-OECD countries. A one-point improvement in the DC pillar score yields an 11.2 per cent improvement in GDP per capita. It is true that achieving a one-point improvement will be much more difficult for an OECD country than a developing country as their DC pillar scores are already high. So, we have evaluated the impact of a one-point DC pillar score change, assuming that the relevant country can achieve that gain in a ten-year period. We therefore assume a 22 per cent GDP per capita improvement above the 1996–2016 trend, and illustrate this below (See Figure 5.3 below). The shaded area represents what has been lost as a result of our failure to address conditions of domestic competition. For the sake of this trend graph, we have ignored exogenous shocks such as the Global Financial Crisis in 2008. We have included another curve that fits the exponential nature of the 1996–2008 trend, plots that trend to 2016 and then assumes a 22 per cent increase in GDP per capita over and above where the best-fit exponential line intersects the y-axis where x=2016. We have also shaded the area under the difference between that point and the best-fit curve. This assumes that a focus on the DC pillar score might have impacted the GFC itself, as much of it can be attributed to market distortions in the fiscal sector.[7] The best-fit curve for 1996–2008 is an exponentially increasing curve, so we have assumed this, identified the intersection point at x=2016 and added 22 per cent GDP per capita to that. The area between the top exponential best-fit curve and the actual curve represents the lost wealth as a result of failure to improve conditions of domestic competition at the same time as improving trade and property rights.

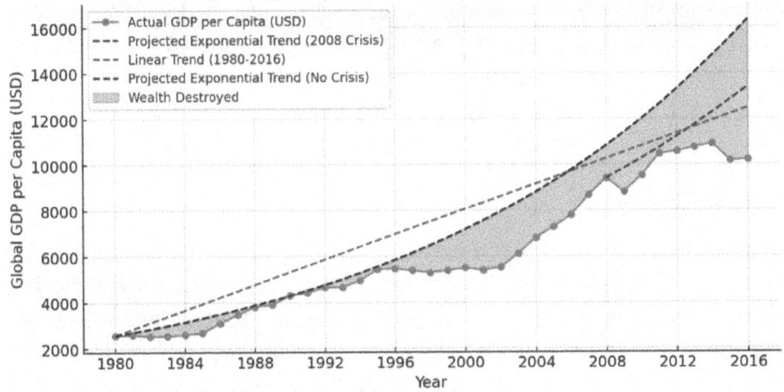

Figure 5.3 Global GDP Per Capita From 1980 to 2016 (Actual, Linear and Exponential Trends)

The scale of these losses is not trivial. The area of the shaded region between 1990 and 2016, representing the amount of wealth destroyed, is approximately 47,781.65 USD·years per capita.

This means that over this 26-year period, each person in the global economy cumulatively missed out on nearly $47,782 in GDP per capita due to deviations from the projected exponential growth trend.

This translates to trillions of dollars of losses to the global economy. Even if we use the red line as the upper bound, the order of magnitude of losses is similar. We can no longer ignore the impact of our failure to deal properly with domestic competition issues, as a vital element of international relations.

The world would look very different today had liberalisation of trade been accompanied by improvement of market competition and property rights protection. Increased GDP per capita growth year on year would enable the major G7 economies to deal with their skyrocketing debt to GDP ratios and would lead to significantly more income for their people.

In such a world of plenty and abundance, resource conflicts would be at a minimum and geopolitical tensions would have been much less. China and Russia would have adopted market-oriented policies instead of being strategically competitive or menacing to G7 interests.

5.3 A Live Experiment Now – the United Kingdom Leaving the European Union

The United Kingdom leaving the EU represents a live experiment in how the different pillar scores of IC, DC and PR can be used to craft a positive outcome or a negative one.

We consider two scenarios. First, where the European Union's DC pillar score is increased by one point – reflecting a situation where the European

Union is moving towards more pro-competitive regulatory frameworks. In the second scenario, we assume that the European Union's DC pillar score is decreasing by one point, reflecting a situation where the European Union is moving towards more anti-competitive regulation.

5.3.1 Scenario 1

In scenario 1, we look at the pre-leaving scenario, where the United Kingdom maintains its DC, IC and PR scores from our model. When it leaves, its IC score will decline to reflect a reduction in trade facilitation elements of the IC score (although not tariff-related elements, as it has not increased its tariff to the European Union and indeed has lowered it to other countries). Applying this to the IC variables, we assume a reduction in trade facilitation score by 0.5, and an increase in tariff related IC variables by 0.3. Since trade facilitation is 57 per cent of the IC pillar score, we assume a 0.285 decline due to trade facilitation decline and a 0.129 increase due to new trade deals, leading to more trade openness for the United Kingdom. The result is a 0.156 decrease in IC score, which correlates to a 0.686 per cent decrease in GDP per capita (a loss of around £220 per person, or a $15bn loss to GDP based on current population). As the European Union improves its DC pillar score by 1, if the United Kingdom follows suit. This leads to an 11.2 per cent increase in GDP per capita (or £3,700 per person). IF the United Kingdom did nothing, it would simply pay the 0.686 per cent GDP per capita loss. In this scenario, the impact of leaving would be +£3,500 per person if it aligned to improving EU DC scores, or -£220 if it did nothing.

5.3.2 Scenario 2

Here, the United Kingdom faces the same trade facilitation loss of 0.686 per cent GDP per capita. But now the European Union has declined its DC score by 1. If the United Kingdom aligns to the European Union's regulatory framework, it too will face a decline of DC score by 1, or 11.2 per cent GDP per capita loss – a total loss of almost £4,000 per person or $274 billion. On the other hand, if the United Kingdom used its newfound regulatory freedom to increase its DC pillar score by 1, that would constitute a £3,724 gain for each person in the United Kingdom. Offset against the loss of £220 due to trade facilitation restrictions, this means that the impact of leaving the European Union is +£3,500 per person. On the other hand, if the United Kingdom dynamically aligns to declining EU DC scores, then the effect of dynamic alignment with the European Union is –£3944.

These two scenarios show us how powerful the DC field score is. The only argument for aligning to EU regulation would be if that regulation is moving in a pro-competitive regulatory direction. If it is not, dynamic alignment would be fatal.[8]

5.4 Potential Resource Conflicts If ACMD Solution Cannot Be Found

If countries continue to distort their markets and ACMDs instead of being tamed, proliferate, then global wealth will be destroyed. As global wealth is destroyed, the poor are plunged into poverty, and this will create social and economic tensions in both developed and developing countries. As competition is forestalled, the cost of key inputs will rise, creating the conditions for resource nationalism and resource conflicts.

Table 5.1 shows the top five locations of a number of critical mineral deposits in the world (measured in metric tons).[9] If these increase in costs, each of these places could become a conflict zone.

We have indicated in bold those countries where there could be conflict involving major powers such as China, Russia and the United States if resources became scarce. Italicized countries would be less likely to enter into conflict, but it is still possible. The countries in plain text are unlikely to be drawn into a conflict. This shows an unhappy coincidence of countries that have significant reserves, which are also likely to become conflict zones if supply becomes constrained.

5.4.1 Ukraine Case Study

Given the current conflict in Ukraine, it is worth looking at the critical minerals that Ukraine has and the impact this has. Ukraine might very well be an example of the kinds of conflicts we will see play out in the future.

Ukraine is one of the most resource-rich countries in Europe with vast deposits of minerals and natural resources that play a crucial role in its economy and industrial base. Ukraine's key resources include the following:

1. **Iron Ore**
    - Ukraine has some of the largest iron ore reserves in the world, mainly concentrated in the **Kryvyi Rih Basin**, **Kremenchuk Basin** and **Bilozerka deposits**.
    - These reserves make Ukraine one of the top producers of iron ore in Europe.
    - The high-quality iron ore is a key input for Ukraine's steel industry.
2. **Coal**
    - Ukraine possesses significant coal reserves, primarily in the **Donets Basin (Donbas)** and **Lviv-Volyn Basin**.
    - The Donbas region, historically a major industrial centre, has been heavily affected by ongoing conflict.
    - Ukraine has large deposits of **anthracite** and **bituminous coal**, essential for energy production and metallurgy.

Table 5.1 The Top Five Locations of a Number of Critical Mineral Deposits in the World

Mineral	*Country 1*	*Country 2*	*Country 3*	*Country 4*	*Country 5*
Lithium	**Chile** (9,300,000; ~44%)	Australia (6,200,000; ~29%)	**Argentina** (3,600,000; ~17%)	China (3,000,000; ~14%)	United States (1,100,000; ~5%)
Cobalt	**DR Congo** (3,500,000; ~51%)	Australia (1,400,000; ~20%)	**Cuba** (500,000; ~7%)	**Philippines** (260,000; ~4%)	Canada (220,000; ~3%)
Nickel	**Indonesia** (21,000,000; ~22%)	Australia (20,000,000; ~21%)	*Brazil* (16,000,000; ~17%)	*Russia* (7,000,000; ~7%)	**Philippines** (4,800,000; ~5%)
Copper	**Chile** (200,000,000; ~23%)	**Peru** (92,000,000; ~11%)	Australia (88,000,000; ~10%)	*Russia* (62,000,000; ~7%)	*Mexico* (53,000,000; ~6%)
Graphite	*Turkey* (90,000,000; ~32%)	*Brazil* (70,000,000; ~25%)	China (55,000,000; ~20%)	**Mozambique** (17,000,000; ~6%)	**Tanzania** (15,000,000; ~5%)
Rare Earth Elements	China (44,000,000; ~36%)	**Vietnam** (22,000,000; ~18%)	*Brazil* (21,000,000; ~17%)	*Russia* (12,000,000; ~10%)	*India* (6,900,000; ~6%)
Platinum Group Metals	**South Africa** (63,000; ~91%)	*Russia* (3,900; ~6%)	**Zimbabwe** (1,200; ~2%)	United States (900; ~1%)	Canada (310; <1%)
Bauxite (Aluminium Ore)	**Guinea** (7,400,000,000; ~24%)	Australia (6,000,000,000; ~20%)	**Vietnam** (3,700,000,000; ~12%)	*Brazil* (2,600,000,000; ~8%)	**Jamaica** (2,000,000,000; ~6%)
Zinc	Australia (68,000,000; ~27%)	China (44,000,000; ~17%)	**Peru** (19,000,000; ~7%)	Mexico (18,000,000; ~7%)	*India* (11,000,000; ~4%)
Manganese	**South Africa** (520,000,000; ~26%)	**Ukraine** (140,000,000; ~7%)	Australia (92,000,000; ~5%)	*Brazil* (54,000,000; ~3%)	China (44,000,000; ~2%)
Chromium	***Kazakhstan*** (230,000,000; ~30%)	**South Africa** (200,000,000; ~26%)	*India* (100,000,000; ~13%)	*Turkey* (74,000,000; ~10%)	Finland (33,000,000; ~4%)
Tin	China (1,500,000; ~30%)	**Indonesia** (800,000; ~16%)	*Brazil* (700,000; ~14%)	**Bolivia** (400,000; ~8%)	**Peru** (310,000; ~6%)

(*Continued*)

Table 5.1 (Continued)

Mineral	*Country 1*	*Country 2*	*Country 3*	*Country 4*	*Country 5*
Tungsten	China (1,900,000; ~61%)	**Vietnam** (95,000; ~3%)	*Russia* (250,000; ~8%)	Canada (290,000; ~9%)	**Bolivia** (53,000; ~2%)
Vanadium	China (9,500,000; ~42%)	*Russia* (5,000,000; ~22%)	**South Africa** (3,500,000; ~15%)	*Brazil* (1,200,000; ~5%)	United States (400,000; ~2%)
Niobium	*Brazil* (16,000,000; ~89%)	Canada (200,000; ~1%)	Australia (100,000; ~0.5%)	*Russia* (50,000; ~0.3%)	**Greenland** (40,000; ~0.2%)
Molybdenum	China (4,300,000; ~38%)	United States (2,700,000; ~24%)	**Chile** (1,800,000; ~16%)	**Peru** (450,000; ~4%)	*Mexico* (200,000; ~2%)
Phosphate Rock	**Morocco** (50,000,000,000; ~70%)	China (3,200,000,000; ~4%)	**Egypt** (2,800,000,000; ~4%)	**Algeria** (2,200,000,000; ~3%)	**Syria** (1,800,000,000; ~2%)
Fluorspar	*Mexico* (68,000,000; ~20%)	**South Africa** (41,000,000; ~12%)	China (24,000,000; ~7%)	**Mongolia** (22,000,000; ~6%)	Spain (6,000,000; ~2%)
Barite	China (37,000,000; ~30%)	*India* (32,000,000; ~26%)	***Kazakhstan*** (16,000,000; ~13%)	*Turkey* (12,000,000; ~10%)	**Morocco** (10,000,000; ~8%)
Potash	Canada (1,000,000,000; ~30%)	*Russia* (600,000,000; ~18%)	*Belarus* (300,000,000; ~9%)	China (100,000,000; ~3%	Germany (90,000,000; ~3%)

Table 5.2 The Top Ten Locations for Energy Reserves in the World

Rank	*Country (Oil)*	*Oil Reserves (Billion Barrels)*	*Country (Natural Gas)*	*Natural Gas Reserves (Trillion Cubic Feet)*	*Country (Coal)*	*Coal Reserves (Billion Short Tons)*
1	**Venezuela**	303	*Russia*	1688	United States	254
2	*Saudi Arabia*	267	**Iran**	1201	*Russia*	176
3	**Iran**	209	*Qatar*	871	Australia	159
4	Canada	164	United States	625	China	141
5	**Iraq**	145	*Saudi Arabia*	333	*India*	106
6	*United Arab Emirates*	113	**Turkmen-istan**	265	Germany	39
7	**Kuwait**	102	*United Arab Emirates*	215	**Ukraine**	34
8	*Russia*	80	**Venezuela**	197	***Kazakhstan***	33
9	United States	55	**Nigeria**	193	**South Africa**	30
10	**Libya**	48	**Algeria**	159	Poland	28

3. **Uranium**
   - Ukraine is one of the few European countries with **domestic uranium production**, primarily in the **Dnepropetrovsk region**.
   - The country has the potential to be more self-sufficient in nuclear fuel supply.
   - Ukraine relies on nuclear power for a significant portion of its electricity.
4. **Manganese**
   - The **Nikopol Basin** is one of the largest manganese ore deposits in the world.
   - Manganese is vital for steelmaking and other industrial applications.
5. **Titanium**
   - Ukraine is one of the leading global producers of **titanium ores**, mainly in the **Zhytomyr and Dnipropetrovsk regions**.
   - Titanium is crucial for aerospace, military and industrial applications.
6. **Graphite**
   - Ukraine has the **largest graphite reserves in Europe**, with major deposits in the **Zavalivske mine (Kirovohrad region)**.
   - Graphite is increasingly in demand for batteries, lubricants and electronics.

7. **Lithium**

   - Ukraine has **significant lithium deposits**, particularly in the **Donetsk, Kirovohrad and Zhytomyr regions**.
   - Lithium is a strategic resource for battery production, making it critical for renewable energy and electric vehicles.

8. **Nickel and Cobalt**

   - Deposits of **nickel and cobalt** are found in the **Kirovohrad and Dnipropetrovsk regions**.
   - These metals are essential for electronics, batteries and high-strength alloys.

9. **Gold**

   - Ukraine has gold deposits in the **Zakarpattia (Carpathian) region** and **Dnipropetrovsk**.
   - Gold exploration has been increasing in recent years.

10. **Oil and Natural Gas**

    - Ukraine has **proven natural gas reserves**, primarily in the **Dnieper-Donets Basin** and the **Carpathian region**.
    - While it imports significant amounts of gas, Ukraine has the potential to increase domestic production.
    - Offshore deposits in the **Black Sea** remain largely untapped (See Table 5.2 above).

11. **Rare Earth Elements (REEs)**

    - Ukraine has **potential rare earth deposits**, which are critical for electronics, defence and renewable energy technologies.

The battle that is going on with regard to Ukraine's resources, which could result in a US–Ukraine agreement on mineral rights exploration as well as Russian territorial expansion claims could be the type of great power conflict we see replay itself in many countries (such as those highlighted earlier) in the future.

As these minerals become more costly to exploit and supply becomes rarer if economic growth is not present, the potential for the type of conflict we see now increases.

While elements are spread across the Earth's crust, they are not evenly **concentrated** in economically viable deposits. Geological processes – like volcanic activity, plate tectonics, sedimentation and hydrothermal activity – cause certain minerals to accumulate in specific locations. For example, while uranium is technically present in trace amounts almost everywhere, rich deposits like those in Kazakhstan, Canada and Australia make extraction much cheaper in those regions.

Exploration costs are a major barrier. Many minerals remain undiscovered simply because surveying and drilling are expensive. With economic growth and technological progress, discovering and exploiting previously uneconomical deposits would become viable.

If growth and investment in R&D continue, new extraction technologies could unlock resources previously considered inaccessible. For example, rich metal nodules containing nickel, cobalt and rare earth elements lie on the ocean floor.

If we want to avoid these conflicts in the future, economic growth is a priority.

5.4.2 Case Study on Semiconductors

We have looked specifically at one area where such tensions might play out is in semiconductor production.

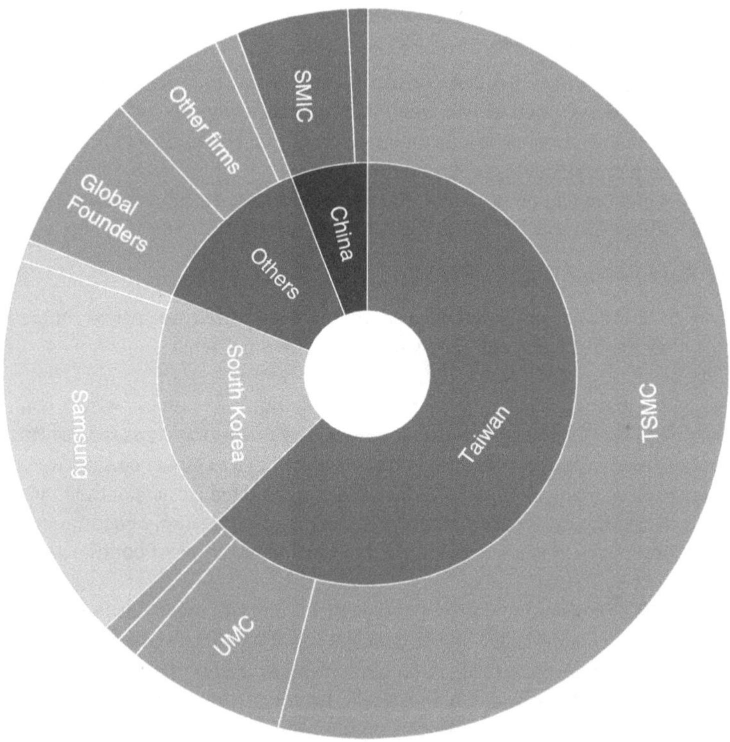

Figure 5.4 Semiconductor Contract Manufacturers by Market Share

The dominance of TSMC in Taiwan can be seen below and this illustrates the high and present risk to the world if there is conflict in the Taiwan Straits (See Figure 5.4 above). It also illustrates the likelihood of such a conflict. Attempts to establish foundries in other countries, especially those most pre-disposed to Western interests, have not been successful for many reasons, but one reason is the difficulty of competing with firms that benefit from ACMDs. The approach which the United States is taking which is to seek to out subsidise China is one that is unlikely to succeed. The United States' debt to GDP ratio is already very high, and any increase in it will put the United States in an even more parlous situation without meaningful growth.

We can therefore see that there are very real-world consequences of a failure to eliminate ACMDs, and thus grow the economy.

5.5 What Can Be Done Now?

Hindsight is always right. But we cannot turn back the clock and correct for what we failed to do in the past. It is therefore imperative that we make the best of the current situation and act quickly to curb the effects of anti-competitive market distortions generally, but specifically and especially in China.

To do this, it will be necessary to be able to quantity the distortion. Without this quantum, it will be very hard to develop a robust defensive mechanism to deal with distortions that stands up to external scrutiny. It is also important that G7 countries adopt similar approaches to the problem and do not adopt a range of different and inconsistent approaches. G7 countries should also develop a mechanism that deals with the actual concerns caused by ACMDs and not be drawn into a debate about the moral rights and wrongs of the Chinese (or indeed any other country's) manner of its internal governance. Countries may govern themselves as they please, but if doing so visits harm on their trading partners, they must compensate them for these harms.

Quantum of Distortion and ACMD Effect on Trade

We have noted above a number of ways in which we can establish the quantum of distortion with regard to its impact on domestic regulation. We now turn to measure that can be introduced to deal with the trade effects of market distortions.

The requirement is for a measure that can be deployed in real time and can be granular enough to support a robust and economically justifiable tariffication. There is a greater sense of urgency for this now as the emerging Trump Tariff Doctrine begins to take shape. President Trump took office in January 2025 and has announced a set of tariff policies that change the geoeconomic tectonic plates.

Notes

1 CEIC Data. *China PMI: Textile Industry: Employment*, available here.
2 Note: The end of MFA allowed several new countries such as Bangladesh to leverage their comparative advantage to become major suppliers to the global garment and textile industry, whereas countries like India with its similar advantages lost out due to poor policy interventions.
3 Source: MeSteel, available here: https://www.mesteel.com/cgi-bin/w3-msql/goto.htm?url=https://www.mesteel.com/info/impo_expo_2011.htm.
4 See, for example, Gersten, D., and Caporal, J. (2020). *Trilateral Group Targets China Industrial Subsidies*. CSIS, available at: Trade Trilateral Targets China's Industrial Subsidies.
5 For a detailed analysis of privatisation in emerging markets, see Singham, Shanker A. (2022). *Market Distortions and Privatisation Processes*. Routledge.
6 See FN 36.
7 See Stockman, David. (2014). *The Great Deformation; The Corruption of Capitalism in America*. Public Affairs; Calomiris, Charles, and Haber, Stephen. (2015). *Fragile by Design: The Political Origins of Banking Crises and Scarce Credit*. Princeton Economic History of the Western World; Rajan, Raghuram. (2011). *Fault Lines*. Princeton University Press.
8 There seems little doubt that the trajectory of EU regulation is in a more anti-competitive direction; see Growth Commission paper 2 for an analysis (available at: GC-Second-Report-The-Impact-of-Regulation-on-Economic-Growth-Sept–2023.pdf); See also Draghi, Mario. *The Future of European Competitiveness*, available at: EU competitiveness: Looking ahead – European Commission.
9 U.S. Geological Survey. (2024). *Mineral Commodity Summaries 2024*. U.S. Geological Survey, 212p, available at: https://doi.org/10.3133/mcs2024.

6 Some Recommendations to Integrate ACMD Policy into Trade and Economic Policy

6.1 Introduction: Application of ACMDs to Trade Policy

Since the late 1940s, two contradictory developments have characterised the international economy. On the one hand, spurred by the memory of the sufferings that protectionism imposed on nations between the two world wars, nations had made a concerted effort to liberalise trade and investment flows across national borders. This has resulted in the spread of general prosperity across nations and in the lifting of hundreds of millions of people above poverty. At the same time, though, there had been a disturbing trend, visible especially since the mid-1980s, of efforts by some countries to free ride on the liberalised global economic regime by distorting trade and investment flows through substantial intervention in their domestic markets to bestow unilateral advantage on favoured domestic firms. Such anti-competitive market distortions (ACMDs) have multiple, deleterious effects on firms, industries and national economies. China has been a particularly egregious violator international norms and it has striven hard, as a matter of state policy, to make Chinese firms globally dominant in industries, especially sunrise ones, in high-technology sectors. This chapter outlines an approach that the United States and the United Kingdom, under the aegis of the New Atlantic Charter, can pursue to bring back order into international economic arrangements. In time, these ideas could be spread to Australia through AUKUS Pillar 2 and Japan. After that, CPTPP and, eventually, WTO disciplines could be agreed.

6.2 Problem Statement

It is important to recognise that ACMDs we highlight in this book are distinctly different from the traditional trade distortions that countries have wrestled with since the beginning of the liberalised trade regime under the auspices of GATT/WTO protocols. Over the years, many countries have sought to distort trade flows across borders for many reasons such as protecting local

DOI: 10.4324/9781003570608-6

employment (such as protection through tariffs, quotas and voluntary restraint agreements), slowing down of the death spiral of uncompetitive industries (steel, textiles and garments) and allowing new or infant industries to grow (through subsidies and tariffs). Over the years, GATT/WTO has developed tools (with varying effectiveness) that deal with these such as classifying subsidies as green, yellow and red to indicate the severity of subsidies used by a country and outlawing the red ones, phasing out yellows, and allowing greens. Granted that there are conflicts among countries as to how to define them and deal with them. Witness the prolonged conflict between United States and European Union over subsidies for the civil aircraft industry. ACMDs, the topic of this book, are different from these traditional trade interventions that affect firms only at the border.

As we have noted elsewhere, the ACMDs we refer to are both trade barriers at the border, property rights violations and market distortions deep within a country that favour some local firms through government laws, regulations and practices that prevent unfettered competition within a country. The heart of ACMD theory is that it unifies these disparate fields. Trade theorists often consider these only in the broadest terms when considering trade interventions such as tariffs and subsidies. Furthermore, such market distortions are not limited to goods, as services are also impacted, as well as mergers and acquisitions and government procurement and investment activities. In addition, distorting countries may benefit from advanced scientific research. Distorters may use a range of ACMDs including intellectual property theft to promote their own scientific research capabilities at the expense of non-distorting countries. These foreign country market distortions, albeit domestic, have enormous impact on international trade flows and thus on foreign players. Clearly, international trade flows are impacted by foreign country market distortions. These impact market access into markets which are distorted. They also give rise to cost reductions among producers which can then out compete other producers in import markets.

International trade agreements, however, have so far not dealt with these kinds of distortions, except those at the border, and then only in terms of effects on producers. A good example of such a predatory ACMD behaviour is China. China has clearly telegraphed its intention to become a leader in a whole range of advanced technology sectors.[1] And it seems to be using the kind of ACMDs we have referred to above in order to gain global dominance in those industries.[2] International trade agreements have so far not dealt effectively with these kinds of distortions. The ACMDs that pervade the China market cannot be disciplined by current trade tools. But whatever tools are used must follow at least the spirit of international trade liberalisation principles (in order to ensure that the United States, United Kingdom and other G-7 countries can maintain the moral high ground with its trading partners), and they must actually be effective in disciplining Chinese behaviour.

6.2.1 Recent Efforts to Address the Problem and Their Inadequacy

In recent years, there have been some efforts to address the ACMD issue in somewhat ad hoc fashion and they have not been very effective.

The first response had been to expand the scope of industrial subsidies. However, these impact only trade in goods and not services, which are significantly affected by ACMDs. A subsidy approach also does not attack the problem at its source, which is the impact of the distortion on competition. We should be concerned about ACMDs because of their effect on competition, which leads to wealth destruction and a negative effect on GDP per capita in a relevant market. The result of ACMDs on certain producers is a by-product. It is affected producers that are likely to complain, but the measure of whether there is a problem should be based on their impact on competition – which is buyers and sellers meeting each other's needs in voluntary exchange.

In addition, the rules governing subsidies are meant for a world where government gives cash to certain firms. In order to countervail them, they need to be specific. However, ACMDs may not be specific and may not therefore qualify as actionable subsidies.

The second approach is to make ad hoc trade deals with China as the first Trump administration sought to do. As we know now, the China deal negotiated by the Trump administration did not succeed in disciplining China distortions in any meaningful manner. Because the Trump tariffs and the Phase 1 deal based on a "forced" market share are clearly contrary to at least the spirit of international trade liberalisation, the US administration also lost the moral high ground for the mechanism proposed.

The third response is for some key countries to collaborate to deal with ACMDs. The WTO trilateral group (European Union, Japan and the United States), for example, has focused on reducing market distortions in third countries. The European Union has come up with a new approach to competition issues, where countries are engaged in market distortions. However, while there was much support for the initiative, the fact that the members are not sufficiently aligned either on the nature of the problem or its solution has meant that little has been accomplished.

Finally, bilateral efforts are being attempted. The Atlantic Charter and G7 announcements in the United Kingdom have both prioritised fair trade and a reduction of market distortions, but there is yet to be flesh on the bones of these proposals. AUKUS Pillar 2 negotiations also potentially could be used to push reduction of ACMDs in markets.

However, none of these developments have attacked the core problem, which is the impact of government distortions on competition in the relevant market. Nor have they suggested remedies, which could actually have a positive impact and stand a chance of changing the behaviour of the distorting countries. The solution proposed in this book intends to resolve the ACMD problem more fully.

6.3 A Proposal to Tackle ACMDs Comprehensively

At the outset, let us be clear. There is no silver bullet that will solve the ACMD problem at one stroke and comprehensively. Instead, the United States, the United Kingdom and other market-oriented economies have to take a series of measures that together can do the following: (1) protect the their markets from the impacts of Chinese and other country ACMDs and (2) incentivise the Chinese and other governments to lower the levels of ACMDs in their market.

Incidentally, there are a few broader purposes for this proposal to tackle ACMDs comprehensively. The first is to create a proactive approach to understanding and dealing with market distortions.[3] The second is to put forward a set of guidelines for countries to act in a consistent way against countries that resort to ACMDs. The third is to serve as an a priori dissuasion mechanism against countries such as China that seek to utilise ACMDs. Finally, this proposal allows countries such as the United States, the United Kingdom and other like-minded market-friendly countries to enshrine key principles of market competition in their trade and investment agreements. In other words, this is both a warning against third-party violators of competition principles and a commitment among the parties to the agreement to sound competition policies.

6.3.1 Levying Countervailing Duties

The simplest response to ACMDs is for countries is to adapt their trade remedy laws to allow for a mechanism where ACMDs, if proven, can be punished by levying a countervailing duty or by "tariffication". This allows the distortion that impacts costs and gives the producers of a distorting market an advantage to be disciplined. However, it does not deal with the situation where that producer has better access in other markets, unless those other countries also operate such a mechanism. It also does not deal with market access issues in the distorting market.

6.3.2 Dealing with ACMDs That Impact Market Access to the Country with ACMDs

Here, the issue is one of equitable access to another country's market when that country is using ACMDs. Here, the ACMD prevents market contestability even where market access if granted.[4]

In addition to disciplines in FTAs that prevent ACMDs in chapters on competition, state aids and subsidies such as in this model text on a market distortions chapter in an FTA.[5] ACMDs in the import market can be disciplined by cross-retaliation including fines, withdrawal of licenses to domestic companies seeking to access other markets [see herein for list of remedies]. Here, the United States, the United Kingdom and other countries should ensure that its trade agreements include specific reference to market distortions offensively, as well as a reference to its defensive measures, which could be unilateral (see sample FTA chapter referred to above).

6.3.3 Dealing with ACMDs That Improve Market Access for Offending Nations

One of the reasons why some countries indulge in ACMDs is to give the companies from that country a leg-up in competition against companies from other countries. For instance, a Chinese firm benefiting from government help through ACMDs may improve their market access to United States leaving local, American firms powerless to match them in cost or competitiveness.

It should be pointed out that China is by no means the only proponent of ACMDs. The Chinese use ACMDs to power their state-led economic model. But, increasingly, we have seen the rise of industrial policy in the United States, the United Kingdom and the European Union. This industrial policy does involve ACMDs. For example, the Inflation Reduction Act (IRA) does distort the global market in favour of US firms.

Inflation Reduction Act-Embedded ACMDs

The **Inflation Reduction Act (IRA)**, signed into law in August 2022, includes numerous provisions aimed at addressing climate change, healthcare costs and corporate taxes. It introduces a number of market distortions some of which are anti-competitive and would constitute ACMDs.

Energy and Climate Subsidies

- **Favouring specific technologies:** The IRA provides significant subsidies for renewable energy technologies like solar, wind and electric vehicles (EVs). These subsidies distort markets by picking winners and losers, potentially crowding out other innovations like nuclear energy, carbon capture or advanced biofuels.
- **Local content requirements:** Tax credits for EVs and renewable energy projects include domestic content requirements, which may increase costs for manufacturers and reduce competition, particularly from international suppliers.

- **Overreliance on tax credits:** The act relies heavily on tax incentives, which can create dependencies, distort price signals and lead to inefficiencies if technologies are not yet cost-competitive.

Healthcare Policies

- **Drug price negotiations:** The IRA empowers Medicare to negotiate the prices of certain prescription drugs. While this aims to lower healthcare costs, it may also distort the pharmaceutical market by reducing incentives for innovation and investment in new drug development.
- **Capping insulin prices:** Price caps on insulin and other drugs can distort the pricing mechanisms and potentially lead to supply shortages if producers find it less profitable to meet demand.

Corporate Minimum Tax

- **15 per cent minimum corporate tax on book income:** This provision targets large corporations that use deductions to lower taxable income. This could disincentivise investment in research and development (R&D) and capital-intensive projects by narrowing the benefits of such deductions.
- **Distortion of financial reporting:** Linking tax policy to book income may incentivise companies to alter financial reporting practices to minimise taxable income, reducing the transparency of financial statements.

Market Overreach

- **Incentivising overcapacity:** Generous subsidies may lead to overbuilding in certain sectors (e.g. wind and solar) without corresponding upgrades in grid infrastructure, creating inefficiencies and misallocated resources.
- **Greenwashing risks:** Subsidies and incentives tied to environmental claims may incentivise companies to exaggerate their sustainability achievements, distorting market competition.

European Green New Deal ("EGD")

The EGD contains a number of market distortions as well.

Energy Policies

- **Subsidising renewable energy**:
  - The EGD allocates significant funding to renewable energy projects (e.g. solar, wind and hydrogen). This creates uneven market conditions, favouring certain technologies while sidelining alternatives like nuclear power or carbon capture technologies.
- **Carbon pricing and Emissions Trading System (ETS)**:
  - The European Union's ETS, a cornerstone of the EGD, imposes carbon costs on emitters. While incentivising decarbonisation, it risks disproportionately affecting energy-intensive industries, leading to carbon leakage (where companies relocate to regions with less stringent climate policies).
- **Energy affordability**:
  - Subsidising green energy while phasing out fossil fuels can lead to increased energy prices for consumers, distorting affordability and competitiveness in energy markets.

Industrial Policies

- **Favouring domestic industries**:
  - The EGD includes measures like the Carbon Border Adjustment Mechanism (CBAM), which imposes tariffs on imports from countries with less stringent climate regulations. While intended to level the playing field, CBAM could distort global trade and disadvantage developing nations, creating geopolitical tensions.
- **Overemphasis on electrification**:
  - Policies favouring electrification (e.g. for transport and heating) could discourage investment in alternative solutions such as synthetic fuels or hydrogen-based systems, reducing technological diversity.

Agricultural and Land-Use Policies

- **Farm to Fork Strategy**:
  - This aims to reduce pesticide use, promote organic farming and cut emissions in agriculture. These policies will lower agricultural productivity, increase costs for farmers and reduce EU agricultural exports, distorting global food markets.
- **Land-use competition**:
  - The EGD incentivises afforestation and bioenergy, potentially competing with agricultural land, driving up food prices and impacting food security.

Financial and Investment Markets

- **Green taxonomy**:
  - The EGD's classification system for sustainable investments seeks to guide capital flows towards green projects. However, some sectors such as nuclear energy and natural gas have faced inconsistent classification. This could distort capital allocation by excluding viable low-carbon solutions.
- **Debt and financial risks**:
  - The European Union's heavy reliance on borrowing through instruments like the NextGenerationEU recovery fund to finance the EGD raises concerns about long-term fiscal sustainability. This could crowd out private investment and distort financial markets.

Social and Regional Disparities

- **Unequal impact on member states**:
  - Wealthier EU nations are better positioned to transition to green technologies, while poorer countries may struggle with the costs. This creates a distorted internal market where competitive dynamics between member states are altered.

Innovation and Competition

- **Regulatory burden**:
  - The EGD introduces extensive environmental regulations and reporting requirements. These can disproportionately impact small and medium-sized enterprises (SMEs) compared to larger firms, distorting competition.
- **Crowding out private innovation**:
  - Public funding and subsidies directed towards specific green technologies may discourage private sector investment in competing or complementary innovations.

Trade and Global Relations

- **Geopolitical tensions**:
  - The EGD's trade-related measures, such as CBAM and sustainability standards, could be perceived as protectionist, straining relationships with non-EU trading partners and distorting global trade.

UK Green New Deal

The **UK Green New Deal (UK GND)** is an ambitious framework aimed at addressing climate change, environmental degradation and social inequality. It focuses on decarbonising the economy, creating green jobs and transitioning to a more sustainable and equitable future. It contains a number of ACMDs.

Energy Transition Policies

- **Subsidising renewables**:
  - Heavy investment in renewables like wind, solar and green hydrogen will distort energy markets by diverting resources from alternative technologies such as nuclear power or carbon capture and storage (CCS).

- **Phasing out fossil fuels**:
  - Rapidly eliminating fossil fuels, such as natural gas for heating, without sufficient infrastructure for alternatives could lead to supply shortages and price volatility, disproportionately affecting low-income households.
- **Overreliance on government support**:
  - Generous subsidies and tax incentives for green energy projects might reduce market competitiveness and innovation, fostering dependency on public funding. The nationalised energy company, Great British Energy, threatens to crowd out private sector investment.

Industrial and Economic Policies

- **Green procurement and subsidies**:
  - Policies that favour domestic green industries, such as electric vehicle (EV) production or offshore wind, may distort market competition by prioritising local over international suppliers, potentially increasing costs for consumers.
- **Carbon pricing**:
  - Expanding carbon pricing mechanisms could disproportionately impact energy-intensive industries, leading to carbon leakage as businesses relocate to countries with lower costs of compliance.
- **Overcentralisation**:
  - The UK GND's reliance on top-down government planning may stifle private sector innovation and create inefficiencies in resource allocation.

Housing and Infrastructure

- **Retrofitting homes**:
  - The UK GND's plans to upgrade housing for energy efficiency (e.g. insulation and heat pumps) could distort construction and

housing markets. Short-term demand spikes may lead to supply bottlenecks, increasing costs and excluding smaller firms.

- **Urban focus**:
    - Investments in public transport and urban infrastructure may disproportionately benefit cities, neglecting rural areas and creating regional disparities in the benefits of the green transition.

Financial and Investment Markets

- **Green bonds and public borrowing**:
    - Significant reliance on green bonds and public debt to fund the UK GND may crowd out private investment, distort credit markets and lead to unsustainable public debt levels.
- **Green taxonomy**:
    - Classifying and regulating "green" investments may exclude viable transitional technologies like natural gas or nuclear, distorting capital allocation and stifling innovation in non-preferred sectors.

Agricultural and Food Systems

- **Sustainable farming initiatives**:
    - Policies to promote organic farming and reduce emissions in agriculture may increase food production costs, raising prices for consumers and reducing the competitiveness of UK agriculture in global markets.
- **Rewilding and land-use changes**:
    - Incentives for rewilding and afforestation could reduce land available for farming, exacerbating food security concerns and distorting rural economies.

Social and Regional Inequalities

- **Unequal impact of green policies**:
    - The cost of transitioning to green technologies (e.g. EVs, heat pumps) disproportionately affects lower income households, which may not benefit equally from subsidies or incentives.

- **Regional disparities**:
  - Regions dependent on traditional industries, such as fossil fuel extraction, may face significant economic dislocation despite the Just Transition Fund, potentially deepening regional inequalities.

Innovation and Competitiveness

- **Picking winners**:
  - Government support for specific sectors or technologies could stifle broader innovation and lead to inefficiencies if supported technologies fail to meet market or environmental expectations.
- **Competition distortions**:
  - Smaller businesses may struggle to compete with large firms that are better positioned to access green subsidies and contracts.

Trade and Global Relations

- **Supply chain vulnerabilities**:
  - The UK GND's focus on localising supply chains for critical materials, such as rare earth elements for EV batteries, may reduce efficiency and increase costs compared to global sourcing.
- **Carbon Border Adjustment Mechanism (CBAM)**:
  - Introducing a CBAM to prevent carbon leakage could strain trade relations, particularly with developing countries, and distort global markets. It also damages GDP per capita for the United Kingdom, as the Growth Commission has noted when it analysed the GDP per capita impact of the United Kingdom following the EU CBAM.[6] It is important to note that the analysis does not examine the underlying conditions such as the Climate Change Act or Emissions Trading Scheme, which are also distortive, but only the impact of the United Kingdom following the EU scheme, all other things being equal.

Developing countries may well argue that the distortions referred to in the above boxes are damaging to them and any mechanism to deal with the problem of ACMDs must take into account the impact of G7 imposed distortions on the rest of the world.

6.4 Remedies

There is a unilateral remedy that could be promulgated by a willing group of allies. This involves identifying the market distortion in the country of export, identifying the effect on competition in a relevant market, and provided the adversely affected firm in the importing country can show causation and damage, then awarding a tariff to, in effect take away the advantage the ACMD conferred on the exporting country producer. While this tariff will help the importing producer who is adversely affected, it is set at a level that will take away the anti-competitive effect, because that is the problem we are concerned about. The damage to the producer in the importing market is a by-product of the ACMD, but the problem the tariff is designed to deal with is the damage to competition, which, as we have shown, leads to a wealth destruction as manifested by a reduction in total GDP per capita – that is, global household income.

A unilateral trade remedy by way of tariffication of the ACMD was set out in the mechanism proposed in the United Kingdom's Trade and Agriculture Commission (see here especially at the Annex where a potential mechanism for dealing with ACMDs is further described). The Trade and Agricultural Commission (TAC) report is significant as the Commission was established by the UK government itself to report on trade and agricultural policy. The report represents a negotiated outcome which was agreed by all interests (NFU, environmental NGOs and importers), which can be implemented in a major G7 country. The ACMD remedial approach proposed here gives an illustration of a mechanism which could be deployed in an FTA where the FTA partner is derogating from a standard agreed in the FTA. However, this does not mean that the overall US policy to distorters should not be significantly more ambitious than this. The Annex describes the TAC use case in more detail. We go on to describe other ways of dealing with ACMDs.

President Donald Trump has issued an executive order to require government departments to assess foreign country unfair trade practices. This is a likely precursor to the use of tariffs, penalties or fines to be applied to countries where these practices are found. This is an opportunity to use an ACMD mechanism such as the one outlined above to discipline these practices, and to ensure that any cost advantages which certain producers receive as a result of them are taken away.

6.5 Dealing with ACMDs That Lower Cost of Foreign Producers and Put Them on a Better Footing in Other Markets: The Need to Act in Concert

Perhaps the most pernicious effect of ACMDs is that they lower the cost of a foreign producer (a favoured company in China, for example) and put it at a competitively advantageous position in other country markets. In such a situation, an effort by one affected country like, say, United Kingdom, to levy countervailing duties (as in Section 4.1) is not effective. The Chinese firm can exploit economies of scale through its operations to other markets, steamroller over rivals in many countries, become a dominant global player and thus be able to survive United Kingdom's countervailing duties. Eventually, no UK companies may be able to compete globally even with the duties. It is critical that United States, the United Kingdom and other countries take this into account while formulating policies against ACMDs introduced by China.

This requires all markets effected to have ACMD mechanisms such as above but which can be used in concert based on a clause in relevant trade agreements where if one country finds an ACMD in place based on its analysis in China, then all other parties to the agreements that contain such a clause can/must apply the tariffication mechanism to producers who benefit from that distortion. This could be done among the Five Eyes countries (FVEY) in the first instance and then broadened out to include the G7 and other regional groupings. Some form of "economic NATO" will be necessary to combat ACMDs and ensure that ultimately the world moves to eliminate them.

This raises an important challenge for countries such as the United States, the United Kingdom and others that want to address the ACMDs of China. If one country, say, United Kingdom, acts against Chinese ACMDs, but other countries do not, then the country that acts (here, the United Kingdom) will pay a heavy price. Worse still, this will allow China to play one country against another and eventually conquer all markets. To paraphrase Benjamin Franklin: If these countries do not hang together, they will assuredly hang separately. We suggest that the key countries such as the United States, the United Kingdom, Japan and others enter into an agreement along these lines. If one of the countries finds that China's ACMDs is affecting the competitiveness of its companies in an industry, it will then report to other countries its findings and ask other countries to act in concert with it against China against those ACMDs. It will then be mandatory on the part of every country party to the agreement to act in unison with the country that proposed action or to publicly announce and explain why it is not accepting that finding and why it is not planning to pursue remedies for the ACMDs so identified. This should be an important part of any agreement on ACMDs since it conveys credible commitments[7] to each other and against other countries which may seek to play a game of divide and conquer.

6.6 Recommendation That Five Eyes Countries Adopt Unilateral Measures

While FVEY countries should prioritise the use of unilateral trade remedy type measures to deal with market distortions and expand their subsidy and tariffication regimes accordingly, they should also prioritise the offensive provisions on ACMDs in their trade agreements with each other and other countries as a matter of urgency. It is likely that these FVEY measures can be put in place more easily because there is more alignment among FVEY member countries. Other areas of potential expansion would include Japan and CPTPP countries (over time). This could be part of a wider commitment to a zone of prosperity that applies ACMD reducing policies.

6.7 Remedies for ACMD Violations

There are a number of remedies that are potentially applicable to ACMD violations as part of unilateral processes. Many of them are drawn from existing trade laws. These include:

1. Tariffication in the case of goods
2. Penalties and Fines
3. Withdrawal of licenses in the case of licensed or regulated services
4. Discipline US companies that receive government distortion benefits
5. Penalties associated with investment decisions through CFIUS-style review processes by adding ACMDs to the list of bars to foreign investment
6. Government procurement bid increase mechanism if the company involved is proven to benefit from a distortion.
7. Removal of ACMD beneficiary country content from Rule of Origin calculation if ACMD is proven.
8. [Other penalties]

In all these cases, the FVEY clause would apply, since the distortion has been proven in one country, it can be accepted to exist for all. In this context, see Section 4.3, which calls on all countries that are party to this agreement against ACMDs to act in concert when one country identifies such ACMDs wherein the burden of proof for not acting falls on other countries.

6.8 Mechanism and Quantum

6.8.1 Goods Tariffication

The mechanism proposed should be an extension of the trade remedy body to include an ACMD issue where an affected party can seek a tariff based on the scale of the anti-competitive harm caused to them by the ACMD itself. In order to satisfy the mechanic:

1. A party must have standing (i.e. must be affected by the ACMD concerned).
2. Evidence of the ACMD in existence (by reference to whether it is a government law, regulation or administrative practice), and whether it has a significant impact on competition. This could include evidence presented in other FVEY markets.
3. Evidence of the competitive harm
4. Evidence of causation
5. Evidence of damage to the party bringing the case

6.8.2 Withdrawal of Licensing for Regulated Services

1. As above, provided that:
2. Harm to competition should be substantial rather than merely significant.
3. Any substantial harm to competition will ground a withdrawal of a licence from the distorting party.

6.8.3 Penalties and Fines

1. As 1 above, provided that:
2. The fines should be calibrated based on the scale of the competitive effect of the distortion.

6.8.4 Public Procurement

The mechanism for increasing bids by a specific amount would follow the mechanism for tariffication with the following provisos:

1. Application by the affected party for an increased percentage for the bid amount based on the ACMD and its anti-competitive effect
2. Temporary measures for time-sensitive bids, subject to posting a bond and review

3. For substantial effects on competition, consider banning the company from the distorting market altogether

6.8.5 Investment

Provisions to ban investment from a company that is benefiting from an ACMD.

1. Adding to CFIUS-type review provisions to pick up ACMDs
2. Ban possible in cases of substantial lessening of competition caused by ACMD in any FVEY country

6.9 Offensive Strategies

There are both offensive and defensive aspects to ACMD theory. Offensively, it is important for countries to affirmatively seek to negotiate a reduction of ACMDs through their international trade arrangements. Modern FTAs do deal with border barriers (tariffs, services access, government procurement, customs and trade facilitation chapters) as well as property rights issues (investment and IP chapters), but they deal inadequately with ACMDs inside the border. Initial forays into this area include competition policy chapters and good regulatory practice chapters, but these do not begin to deal with the entirety of the internal market problem. We have developed a sample chapter on competition, SOEs and market distortions that would be suitable for inclusion in a trade agreement (see Competere-Sample-Chapter-Report-Final.pdf).

However, offensive measures are addressing barriers in markets to exporters – the sorts of things that deny contestability even if access is granted in other parts of the agreement.[8] We need to also address actions taken in one market that give exporters an unearned cost advantage in other markets (because costs are artificially reduced by distortions). In this context and indeed in the offensive one, it must be noted that almost everything the government does is a distortion, but that does not mean it is anti-competitive or not. By using competition effects as the yardstick by which we judge government action, we are concerned only with those market distortions that damage competition in a relevant market (and thus destroy wealth in that market). The relevant market may be the global market, the importer market or some broader geographic market. It may include the product which gains the benefit of the market distortion, or it may include all products that compete with it. In this respect, the analysis is a standard competition policy analysis. This is appropriate as the overall goal of ACMD theory is to reduce ACMDs in all markets and so create wealth. How that wealth is distributed is determined by billions of voluntary exchanges between willing buyers and sellers undistorted by ACMDs.

6.9.1 Application to Third Countries, Especially Developing Countries

Many countries maintain quota arrangements with the largest markets in the world typically among the G7. The European Union, the United Kingdom and the United States all have some form of similar arrangement. However, if China or other major distorters can access those larger markets without some form of ACMD defensive mechanism, then they will quickly lose their ability to be competitive in these markets. Hence, one additional mechanism is to allow countries to maintain preferences, which would otherwise be lowered (this would have dealt with the issue raised with the China WTO accession and the expiration of the MFA referred to in Chapter Five. As G7 countries move towards mechanisms, which are based on free trade agreements and economic partnership agreements with developing countries, it will be important to recognise that ACMDs in one country can give producers in that country an edge over producers from developing countries, and this requires a solution in the international trading system.

6.10 Quantum

The precise measurement of the ACMD is obviously critical and controversial. By using a competition metric and an adversarial process, this allows the private sector to do the work to develop the justification for the tariff sought, which could be used to offset the advantage conferred by the ACMD. We have shown how the quantum of distortion could be calculated but by shifting the burden of proof onto the aggrieved private sector firm who can prove the key elements of an ACMD under 4.7.1 above as they wish. It would be up to the tribunal concerned to determine whether a case had been satisfactorily proven. This is similar to private antitrust litigation where it is not stipulated anywhere that a plaintiff must use a particular type of metric. There are many methods that complainants can use including the likely effect on competition (proxying the distortion to the impact of a merger on competition, for example).

However, tribunals should have the statutory power to launch sua sponte investigations with their own evidence of distortion. There are many ways of showing the anti-competitive effect of a distortion just as there are many ways of showing this effect in competition analysis. The econometric model highlighted earlier gives a sense of the GDP per capita impact of distortions for a given country, but a competition-based metric is necessary to show the competitive damage done by a specific ACMD.

6.11 Handling ACMDs: UK Use Case

Developing a Trade Policy Mechanism to Address New Problems in International Trade: UK Trade and Agriculture Commission Proposal Use Case

6.11.1 Overview

In 2021, the UK Trade and Agriculture Commission (TAC) issued a report which, among other proposals, recommended a novel trade mechanism to deal with anticompetitive market distortions that harm international trade and undermine efforts to promote economically beneficial trade liberalisation. This mechanism provides a possible solution to address new challenges that confront nations in trade negotiations. This mechanism is discussed later.

6.11.2 A Tariffication Mechanism to Deal with New Problems

The TAC has proposed the following mechanism to deal with the issues outlined earlier.

It proposes a tariffication of distortion mechanism, which could be used in trade policy to deal with situations where countries agree to lower their tariffs but protect their markets and give their producers an artificial edge by distorting their markets through ACMDs.

The result of the mechanism is a tariff based on the scale of the distortion which operates like a trade remedy. The mechanism can also be used offensively where a country is preventing market access for the exporting country through the ACMD or, defensively, where an ACMD in a foreign market leads to excess exports from that market.

The TAC proposal is an example of the tariffication method at work.

6.12 Details of the Mechanism and Its Application

6.12.1 Offensive Measures

We could envisage provisions on ACMDs in trade agreements that discipline their use, and allow dispute resolution when they are applied in violation of the agreement.

6.12.2 Defensive Measures

An aggrieved country would have to show:

- An ACMD (i.e. deviation from an agreed standard inserted into an FTA or other trade agreement)
- An impact on competition
- Excess exports as a result of the distortion
- Damage to the aggrieved nation's producers

In addition to the cases above, an ACMD could result from the deliberate derogation from a country's own law in order to promote trade or competitive advantage.

The questions to be resolved would be as follows:

- Is there an international standard which covers the issue?
- Is country X deviating from that standard for trade or competitive advantage?
- Is there an effect on trade and competition? To match other GATT provisions, this could be an equality of competitive opportunity test.
- Are there excess exports from country X into country Y as a result?
- Are country Y's producers adversely affected and can you prove both damage and causation?
- If yes to all, then the tariffication mechanism can be applied.

6.12.3 Some General Observations

The tariff would be calibrated to the scale of the ACMD and would apply only to the product category in which the distortion is occurring. The advantage of this over a more conventional trade remedy is that it is based on cost as opposed to price, and is designed to remove the effects of the distorting activity. It would not be applied on a retaliatory basis in other unrelated sectors. The innovation here is that the scale of the tariffication would not be correlated to the alleged damage to the producer but to the damage to the relevant product market. The remedy seeks to get at the wealth destroyed out of the economy which is proxied by GDP per capita (less government spending).

The TAC proposal is to use this mechanism to deal with distortions in order to maintain a commitment to zero tariffs and zero quotas in agriculture, a notoriously difficult piece of trade liberalisation but crucially important for international trade.

The mechanism seeks to ensure that where countries derogate from commitments made in FTAs or ultimately internationally in the WTO, and do so for trade and competition advantage, there is a real means to discipline them through the application of a tariff. But the TAC proposal also looks at the offensive agenda and how disciplines on ACMDs can be used to limit trade barriers in other markets as part of the United Kingdom's FTA agenda.

We find this mechanism to be highly commendable as a way of dealing with defensive issues without the dangers of an ex-ante dual tariff and the protectionist concerns that could result.

6.13 Potential to Use ACMD Mechanism Offensively to Deal with Government Distortions That Block the Aggrieved Country's Exports

Where an ACMD is being used to protect a particular domestic industry, using the ACMD mechanism to apply a tariff for the exports of that industry would help, but this may not apply where the purpose is protective, and the industry does not export much. In this case, it would be important to ensure that FTAs include disciplines on these ACMDs, which, if breached, could lead to dispute settlement and the potential for retaliatory tariffs for sectors of the culpable trading partner that do export. This is certainly normal WTO-sanctioned practice and could be used here to encourage compliance. It is clear from the experience in dealing with countries that engage in ACMDs for trade or competition advantage that unless there are robust disciplines, mere hortatory language would accomplish little or nothing.

The mechanism is applicable generally to a broad array of trade negotiations:

The mechanism has far broader implications than the UK trade policy. It could be a much more nuanced solution to the current US–China disputes, one which would not be as damaging for global trade as national security-based tariffs, but would recognise the fact that the impact of Chinese market distortions on global trade is severe.

This type of mechanism could also feed into the work of the trilateral group on market distortions in the WTO and be a complement to existing measures allowed under the Agreement on Subsidies and Countervailing Measures.

6.14 The Impact of ACMDs in Other Areas

We have mentioned government procurement, licensing in the case of services, but the impact of ACMDs in a market must also be considered in private competition or antitrust analysis. This is particularly true in the case of allegations of predatory conduct by entities. Historically, the Brooke Group case makes it clear that predatory conduct can only be imputed if prices are below some measure of cost.[9] This is because merely discriminatory pricing is both pro-competitive and if done by a party without market power will merely result in that party losing money and potentially going out of business itself, but presents no threat of market exit of other participants. However, these arguments are turned on their head in the case of a government, which is a revenue maximiser at best. A company benefited by Chinese ACMDs, for example, can sustain below-cost pricing for considerable periods of time, long enough to drive competitors out of the market.

ACMDs should also be considered in merger policy. The likelihood of a merger substantially lessening competition is much, much greater in cases where one of the parties benefits from ACMDs as it increases the potential for predatory behaviour post-merger. The Bundeskartellamt looked at this in the context of the merger between CRRC and Vossloh.

As the OECD has noted[10]

> This case pertained to the acquisition of Vossloh Locomotives GmbH ("Vossloh") by Chinese state-owned company CRRC Zhuzhou Locomotives Co., Ltd. ("CRRC Zhuzhou Locomotives"). Vossloh is a leading rail technology company focused on rail infrastructure, while CRRC Zhuzhou Locomotives is a subsidiary of CRRC Corporation (CRRC). CRRC is listed and is 51 per cent owned by the Chinese State. CRRC is the world's largest manufacturer of rolling stock. In its merger assessment, the BKa thoroughly examined the particularities associated with the acquisition of the European market leader by a resource-rich SOE from a centrally controlled national economy. It considered the impact of possible state subsidies, the availability of technical and financial means and strategic advantages from other shareholdings (CRRC, through several other subsidiaries, plays an important role in China's industry strategies) in the competitive assessment of the merger. This included an analysis of the threat of low-price and dumping strategies and the cost advantages resulting from CRRC's state-subsidised activities in many other markets – including its vertical integration, financial resources resulting from de facto or de jure monopoly on its home market(s), explicit government promotion and favourable input prices. It was argued by the BKa that, while low pricing strategies in the short run are "inherently competitive" and benefit consumers, such low pricing strategies would need to be grounded on comparative cost advantages of the company concerned vis-à-vis its competitors. If, however, the low pricing strategies are a result of systematic subsidisation, they can distort competition and lead to serious market distortions in the long run. Ultimately, the existing concerns – the considerable financial resources of the acquirer and the resulting potential for anti-competitive conduct in the future – did not justify a prohibition, as Vossloh's competitiveness had considerably deteriorated over the last few years and CRRC had only been a small player on the European market until then. This case shows that while SOEs may enter markets with substantial economic power, this does not necessarily pose a threat to effective competition. It also shows, however, that financial strength can be a factor of importance for the assessment of a merger, even if it may not be the determining factor (see below under lesson nr. 3).
>
> Source: Bundeskartellambt B4-115-19 CRRC/Vossloh and Bundeskartellamt, press release, 27 April 2020; Chinese company CRRC can acquire Vossloh's shunter division.

A number of cases in the postal sector have dealt with anti-competitive activities by SOEs where there is regular competition between private express delivery operators and largely state-owned postal companies. The OECD report (see above) notes:

> At the end of the 1990s and beginning of 2000, many countries witnessed a large liberalisation and privatisation wave in the postal sector. Consequently, this sector is one in which SOEs are in constant competition with private companies, or private companies are operating on both reserved markets (monopoly) and markets open to competition. Concerns often arise surrounding the potential anticompetitive behaviour in the competitive segments of the postal sector by incumbent postal operators which benefit from exclusive privileges. These concerns particularly relate to anti-competitive cross subsidisation or predatory pricing. On one hand, relatively limited barriers to entry in the postal sector may limit the likelihood of predatory pricing by profit-maximising firms. On the other hand, limited or restricted incentives for profit maximisation by regulated or SOEs may increase the incentive for the incumbent to cross-subsidise. Many countries have established independent regulatory authorities for the postal sector.[11]

UPS brought a case against Deutsche Post for anti-competitive cross-subsidisation in which these issues were raised. In the 2001 case, the European Commission ruled that Deutsche had illegally used profits from its monopoly to deliver letter as means of subsidisation to its prices for business parcels and packages. The postal service was intercepting, surcharging and delaying incoming international mail. The ruling in favour of United Postal Services (UPS) was a first landmark ruling where regulators attacked cross-subsidies by European postal services. The Commission condemned Deutsche Post AG for having adopted anti-competitive practices, which largely included fidelity rebates and predatory pricings in the market.[12] The Commission also clarified under which below-cost pricing charged by a monopoly would be abusive and illegal under competition rules. And as such, the Commission is working closely with the National Competition Authorities to identify practices of competitive abuses in the postal services.

6.15 A Partial Solution

The difficulty in mechanisms to deal with distortion is the need to prove that the distortion had an anti-competitive effect in a relevant product or geographic market. We have noted earlier that the antitrust economic and legal literatures provide ample ways to measure a substantial lessening of competition. It will be necessary to determine what is the relevant product and geographic market.

It would seem sensible to consider the market in which the aggrieved party resides to be the relevant geographic market, but this is not straightforward as consumers might benefit from new entrants in other geographic areas if activities by the ACMD beneficiary caused market exit of firms in the country of the complainant damaged firm. Lessening of competition will be harder to prove in a global market. But lessening of competition in the global market will clearly have an impact on GDP per capita in the world and therefore provide a rigid underpinning for any action taken against the distorter.

6.16 Impact of Quantum Computing on Calculation Methods

Since Krugman initially wrote on the subject of domestic distortions in the 1980s, there has been a massive increase in supercomputing power, and now the advent of quantum computing and machine learning/AI. These new tools have a role to play in helping us to get a better understanding of the quantum of distortion.

It is possible to model competing supply chains as if it is a complex biological system. By applying a distortion at the node, we can model the effects of distortions on the system to see whether there is a lessening of competition, and a negative effect on trade.

We have discussed the basic econometric models we have been using to measure distortion starting with the SRB model and its various iterations (SRB-β and SRB-γ).

We have also discussed the agency-based model that we developed with colleagues from the Centre for Economics and Business Research (Cebr).

The new model we are investigating uses the results of SRB-γ and applies them to a probabilistic and not deterministic model, which is more in keeping with the actual experience of economic transactions which are a series of voluntary exchanges between buyers and sellers who move around in space until they interact. In this vision, the interactions between buyers and sellers can be analogised to probabilistic interactions consisting of a potential and kinetic term given to these voluntary exchanges by the forces which are applied to the buyers and sellers. In keeping with the SRB models, we assume that there are three forces that impact these entities which are analogised as particles whose distribution in space is given by a wavefunction. These forces, as in the econometric models, are IC (trade openness), DC (domestic competition) and PR (property rights protection). We assume that these forces imbue our "particles" with potential energy (which, we assume, is the potential for wealth creation), and kinetic energy (which reflects the rate of change of momentum of the particles indicating the intensity of any interaction between them). So, as the IC, DC and PR field scores decline, more distortions are introduced, which makes that delta much smaller, and less wealth is created from these interactions.

We have discussed in Chapters 3 and 4 new approaches to economic modelling based on econophysics (agency-based modelling) and similar approaches drawn more from the physical sciences. The model could also be used to model the negative impact of ACMDs on a two or n-party system and therefore could be grounds for a tariffication mechanism to be applied.

6.17 Application of Quantum Tool to ACMD Trade Tariffication

In Chapters 3 and 4, we discussed the model as applied to a one-country system. The model would give us an indication of the wealth creation impact of any policy, law or administrative action, which would lead to a reduction in the three pillars of IC, DC and PR (and therefore lower their potential "energy"). We can apply this model to a two-body problem. Consider country A and B who trade with each other. Country A imposes an ACMD, which reduces its DC pillar score. This gives its producers a cost advantage over producers in country B.

We have foreshadowed a way of measuring distortion using quantum formalism. We are by no means the first to look at applying quantum methodology and formalism to problems outside of the domain of particle physics. Economists have used thermodynamics and statistical mechanics in the past, and biologists and psychologists have used quantum techniques to look at human interactions. This is the first attempt to apply quantum formalism in the context of ACMDs and their effect on voluntary exchange.

6.18 Recent Developments: Trump Administration

At the time of writing, there have been significant developments as President Trump came into office. Trade policy has been a key focus of the administration, and an emerging Trump Tariff Doctrine is beginning to take shape. This consist of three main strands. First, there are tariff threats to secure non-trade actions from trading partners. This includes the 25 per cent tariff threatened on Mexico and Canada to ensure that both countries focus attention on the problem of fentanyl distribution in the United States and the problems with immigration at the US border. It also includes the threat of tariffs on Colombia when it refused entry of planes carrying illegal migrants deported from the United States. These tariffs were also never applied as Colombia backed down quite quickly. Strand 1 tariffs are either never imposed or very short lived. Strand 2 tariffs are relatively low tariffs imposed across the board for revenue purposes. A 5 per cent tariff across the board would raise $180 billion in revenue and would likely be responded to with a small appreciation of US currency and small depreciation in foreign currencies, meaning that supply chains would not reorient much. This is then quite attractive to the administration to "pay for" tax cuts. It would be preferable to fund tax cuts with economic growth. The third strand is the most important for the purpose of this book – this relates to reciprocal tariffs where foreign countries have less open trade regimes than the United States (higher tariffs), less competitive regulation (regulatory barriers or other ACMDs that harm US firms) or violate US firms' property rights (such as investment rules or intellectual property violation). In a sense, the US government seeks to tarifficate ACMDs in the way we have suggested in this book. We can summarise the Strand 3 approach as below.

6.18.1 Trade Policy Recommendations on Foreign Country Unfair Trade Practices

On January 20, President Trump issued a Memorandum on America First Trade Policy. The AFTP Memo directed executive departments and agencies to issue reports to him by April 1 on actions the new administration could take to address specific international trade problems.

One major problem highlighted by the Memo is unfair foreign government practices that harm US trade. These have been particularly pervasive in China and existing trade remedies such as anti-dumping and countervailing duty law are not designed to deal with systemic distortions on the China scale.

This Memorandum has now been supplemented by the President's memorandum and executive order regarding reciprocal tariffs.

These two memoranda outline the emergence of a Trump Trade Doctrine, which recognises that trade policy must now take into consideration not only border measures and tariffs but also conditions of domestic competition, regulatory barriers and property rights protection – in short, measures internal or external that have an adverse impact on US firms. President Trump intends to calibrate the US tariff based on all these factors.

This memo provides a legal and economic underpinning the Trump Trade Doctrine and suggests how that tariff might be arrived out. It also suggests a new remedy for ongoing complaints that US firms have regarding practices in other countries that have an adverse effect on trade.

6.18.2 Anti-Competitive Market Distortions Are an Unfair Trade Practice

The United States maintains anti-dumping laws to deal with goods that have lower prices in the US market than the home country or other appropriate market. It maintains countervailing duty laws to deal with specific subsidies, but this mechanism was really designed where governments give money to a specific firm. Many of the market distortions, which are promulgated by the United States' trade partners, are not specific and apply across whole sectors. They also have damaging effects on competition in relevant markets, which is important given the proven effect on GDP per capita of anti-competitive regulatory systems. Many of these measures are therefore outside the scope of traditional trade remedy laws.

We have provided a framework in a number of papers and books, which could be useful to the Trump administration in examining these issues.[13] The framework posits that there are a series of ACMDs, which include the following relevant to the Trump administration's Executive Order:

1. A country charges higher tariffs than the United States does (i.e. is less open to trade than the United States); or
2. Distorts its market with regulatory barriers that keep US goods out or artificially lowers the costs of competing firms (a measure of domestic competition); or
3. A country does not protect property rights including intellectual property rights

We believe that it is necessary to differentiate between government actions, policies and practices that distort markets in ways that artificially reduce the costs of US trading partner firms exporting to the United States or third countries, such as those above from the ordinary working out of the laws of comparative advantage. It is only ACMDs that should be actionable by US firms or by the US government.[14]

ACMDs have an undeniable impact on trade. They damage competition and thus lower GDP per capita in the home market as well as export and global markets. Left to proliferate, they threaten the ability of US producers to be successful around the world. Our proposal aims to take away any trade advantage they offer, and also to give an incentive for their promoters to lower their use.

6.18.3 What Is an ACMD?

Anticompetitive market distortions analysis provides a lens and potential framework for combating unfair trade practices.

ACMDs are described in a November 2024 report by the non-partisan Growth Commission, presenting economic policy advice for President-Elect Trump:

> "ACMDs involve government actions that empower certain private interests to obtain or retain artificial competitive advantages over their rivals

> be they foreign or domestic. In particular, ACMDs may flow from government regulations that eliminate or lessen competition, regulations that apply differently to different firms, and regulations that exempt certain favored firms from coverage".

ACMD analysis may yield precise cost estimates that are helpful to the United States in bilateral trade negotiations centred on unfair practices, as well as in the implementation of any unilateral remedy.

6.18.4 A Tariff (and/or Other Measures) May Be Justified in the Case of an ACMD

ACMDs damage trade and harm US producers and the wider US economy because of their wealth destructive impacts. A tariff to remove the advantage conferred on foreign producers in the United States and other markets is therefore a needed corrective to deliver a level playing field for competition.

6.18.5 Addressing Unfair Trade Practices

Section 2(c) of the AFTP Memo directs the US Trade Representative to "undertake a review of, and identify, any unfair trade practices by other countries and recommend appropriate actions to remedy such practices under applicable [legal] authorities".

One key legal authority (19 U.S.C. section 2411) authorises the Trade Representative to impose duties, fees or other restrictions on imported goods and services in response to unfair practices.

It also empowers the Trade Representative to enter into foreign agreements with offending countries to (1) eliminate, or phase out, an unfair act, policy or practice; (2) eliminate any burden or restriction on US commerce resulting from such act, policy or practice; or (3) provide the harmed US industry with satisfactory compensatory trade benefits.

Unfair trade practices (referred to as "unreasonable" under the statute) are defined to include a broad set of foreign government practices that distort competitive trade. These include, for example, actions that artificially favour foreign exports, deny non-discriminatory market access for US firms, harm US competitors' IP rights and otherwise involve foreign government toleration of systematic anticompetitive activities.

The United States should include a tariff response to ACMDs in foreign markets by enhancing the existing trade remedy bodies to include an ACMD mechanism (currently ITA in Commerce and the International Trade Commission). Additionally, the views of the FTC should be solicited regarding the competition harm.

6.18.6 Tariffication of ACMDs

Potential tariffication of ACMDs has been suggested by President Trump and is the most controversial area. The challenge is the use of a tariff that lowers the United States' IC pillar score in an effort to improve the IC, DC and PR scores of trading partners. If those other countries simply retaliate as seems likely in an effort to persuade the United States to remove its tariff, then both parties will have lowered their IC scores, and DC and PR scores may not change. On the other hand, if the result is the improvement of the DC and PR scores, such that the US and trading partner tariffs return to the status quo ante, then net GDP per capita will have increased. This is the best outcome. President Trump is betting that the size and attractiveness of the US market will drive this change. In this context, we note that a reduction in IC scores has much less of an effect than the size of the DC and PR pillar scores. In other words, IC and PR improvements would more than compensate from an IC reduction.

Assuming it can be an effective tool to accomplish global improvements in ACMD reduction, tariffication is possible using the ACMD economic model developed in this book. The ACMD model assigns a pillar score to each country under the three areas that the Trump administration is investigating (i.e. trade openness, domestic competition in regulation and property rights protection). These allow us to estimate the impact of changes in this area. For example, if we increase these scores to optimised levels, we can identify the GDP per capita gains a country might get, as a result of improving these to levels where there is no trade effect on the United States. It is in the country's own interests to do this, but as long as their scores are not optimal, they are having a negative impact on trade with the United States. The percentage change could be correlated to a suitable tariff the United States could charge.[15] The rationale for this is that these ACMDs not only damage a domestic economy but also have impacts on international trade.

To achieve a truly reciprocal result, the exercise could be repeated optimising the country's scores to US levels. In cases where a country is already at US levels, no tariff would apply.

We now consider two worked examples including China and Germany. The methodology we use is to compare countries' scores from the ACMD index, which allows us to correlate changes in pillar scores with GDP per capita.[16] Since these pillars all have an impact on trade, we correlate these with a tariff that would be needed, if the domestic GDP per capita impact is correlated with the damage being done to US firms.[17]

By reference, US pillar scores are:

IC = 4.7
DC = 5.9
PR = 5.52

China's pillar scores are as follows:

IC = 4.4
DC = 4.4
PR = 4.13

Therefore, to equal the United States, China would have to improve its IC score by 0.3 (0.66 per cent GDP per capita gain), its DC score by 1.5 (a 16.5 per cent GDP per cap gain) and its PR score by 1.39 (a 10.56 per cent GDP per capita gain). The total gain in GDP per capita of holding the United States constant and improving China to US levels would be a 27.72 per cent gain in GDP per capita system wide.

Germany's pillar scores are

IC = 5.5
DC = 5.4
PR = 5.3

To achieve US levels, Germany needs to only improve its DC and PR pillar scores by 0.5 and 1.2 respectively. This yields 14.62 per cent.

This does not mean that the tariff should be equal to this loss, but it would be economically justified to claim that such a tariff is directly linked to the damage that the trading partner is doing to the GDP per capita (a measure of wealth creation) over the combined US + trading partner region.

There is a challenge with developing countries whose impact on US firms and US consumers is generally slight. The Trump administration could adopt a mechanism similar to special and differential treatment in the WTO by exempting these countries from any tariffs on the basis of their limited trade effect, reserving the tariff for larger countries.

The US tariff could then be lowered as countries improve their pillar scores.

It is likely that larger countries will retaliate against such actions. The usual method of retaliation is to select products that have particularly important political impacts.

6.18.7 A Defensive Trade Remedy

In addition, individually affected firms should be given a remedy. The core defensive trade remedy is to apply a tariff that is linked to the impact of the ACMD ("ACMD Tariffication"), and thus penalise the producer who benefits from unfair advantage in its export markets.

With respect to services, the trade remedy must provide the equivalent of an ACMD Tariffication, understanding that services cross borders in a very different way from goods. The United States already has trade laws that with some adaptation could be used to combat distortions.

The anti-distortion trade remedy measure should operate in the following way:

1. An injured party would bring a complaint to the trade remedy agency;
2. The injured party would have to prove that there was an ACMD in a relevant market; this would include proving the following elements: a. A distortion; b. an anti-competitive effect with respect to consumer welfare; c. Harm to the injured party caused by the distortion;
3. The defendant would be allowed to adduce exculpatory evidence;
4. A decision would be made on ACMDs and tariffication (or equivalent for services) of distortion;
5. An appellate process would follow;
6. Finally, there would be a review process in which the defendant could prove that the distortion had been eliminated at any time.

There are many industries that benefit from ACMDs that damage competition. One example is large-scale commercial aircraft production. Damaged US producers could bring cases to address China's ACMDs by applying for a tariff linked to the scale of the ACMD. The US producer could adduce evidence of the distortion and its effect on the market for the production of large-scale commercial aircraft. Given the limited number of producers, the impact of the China ACMD in this area is likely to significantly lessen competition. Causation and damage could then be proved. The advantage of this type of remedy is that affected parties are motivated to gather the evidence and prove the case.

The difference between this and traditional trade remedies is that the focus here is the impact on competition of the ACMD. This is important because it is this competition harm that destroys wealth and lowers GDP per capita in the relevant market.

6.18.8 Translating This into Trade Policy

We have envisaged a unilateral remedy that the United States could adopt. The United States should also include an ACMD chapter in its trade agreements building on the competition and SOE chapters in the USMCA, for example. The attached link contains a sample chapter in an FTA (Competere-Sample-Chapter-Report-Final.pdf.). Other countries with whom the United States has trade deals should be required to adopt similar approaches to China as the United States does. Such an approach does also raise an interesting question for other countries. All countries are damaged by the ACMDs of their trading partners. It is open to countries to adopt their own versions of a tariffication based on the ACMDs of their partners. While this carries risk on increased global trade barriers, it also carries the potential for a ratcheting down of ACMDs globally, which would lead to a significant potential increase in GDP per capita globally. In many ways, this replicates the initial reciprocal tariff reduction envisaged by Cordell Hull in the 1930s and put into practice in the GATT 1947.[18] That system facilitated progressive trade liberalisation by negotiating between principle suppliers and principle consumers and spreading that deal to all parties through most favoured nation. In this case, the threat of increasing the tariff is used to systematically ratchet down ACMDs across the globe.

Given what we have said about the consequences of failure to reduce ACMDs, and the impact that their proliferation is having on global growth rates, this may represent a way to actually course correct the global economy. It should be broadly welcomed.

6.19 Conclusion

ACMDs are a systemic barrier to global prosperity. They matter to the countries that impose them by generating inefficiency and destroying wealth out of their economies. ACMDs can also be used as weapons by countries to damage producers in their trading partners eviscerating the gains of trade and visiting harm on the global economy. Both these effects operate together as a vicious circle to push people into poverty and eliminate opportunity for new businesses and consumers alike. They can turn formerly successful economies into dead zones where entrepreneurs have no hope for the future. And because they are ungoverned spaces, they leave countries that are harmed by them no choice but to retaliate with sanctions and measures that are often worse than the disease they intend to cure. This creates further momentum to the vicious cycle, plunging the world into ever more darkness and poverty.

We have established that these effects are not small effects, but imperil at least three or four times the level of GDP losses than more conventional trade barriers at the border. We have established that there are ways of quantifying them and reducing them. A calibrated tariffication-based mechanism to address ACMDs could be used flexibly for offensive and defensive purposes. Such a mechanism represents the type of problem solving and innovative thinking that the international trading system needs as it faces a range of challenges that threaten liberalisation itself and the hard-won gains of the post-war GATT/WTO system.

That we have done so little to deal with them is an indication of the failure of our own policymaking. We have had ample warning. Given the huge geopolitical stakes at play now, continued failure in this vital area can only be deemed to be gross negligence. We have shown that the failure to deal with these issues leads inexorably to a rise in nationalism and protectionism as domestic producers demand protection from foreign country unfair practices, which, they rightly argue, their own policymakers have done little about. While we cannot turn back the clock to 1989, and deal with all these issues at the time they started to arise, leading us to the End of History and not the Clash of Civilisations, we can work to correct this ex post. We have suggested both offensive and defensive mechanisms for doing so. We have illustrated with a series of economic models that measurement of these distortions is feasible. We have foreshadowed an entirely different approach drawn from the physical sciences that can pick up the dynamic losses caused by ACMDs much more successfully than we have been able to do before. I do not suggest that the elimination of ACMDs will solve all the world's problems. There are many conflicts not rooted in economics, but they are actually comparatively few. And it is economic forces that sustain the armies of people who are drawn into such conflicts as they often perceive that the ideology they have chosen to support stands against an ideology that offers them nothing. It is the interplay of economic forces that are at the root cause of much global conflict. If we understood them and were able through sound policy to channel them in such a way as to create wealth, much of that conflict would become irrelevant. I do not pretend that ACMD elimination will end all wars, but it will do much to stop many from ever arising and shorten the ones that do.

Get this wrong, and our children to whom we leave a world much poorer and more violent than we found it will not forgive. Nor should they. Their future is entirely in our hands.

Will we look forward to a world where the prosperity of the post war period increases into Churchill's sunlit uplands of prosperity and peace, or will we look back a generation hence a little wistfully at this remarkable period in human history between 1947 and 2006 of growth and prosperity and say this was an aberration in the general human condition of conflict and poverty? The answer to that question and the hopes of billions of the world's citizens is in our hands. Let us not drop this chalice.

Notes

1 Made in China 2025 Explained, A Guide to Understanding China's Next Wave of Innovation, China Innovation Project, Harvard University, Newsletter, available at: https://projects.iq.harvard.edu/innovation/made-china-2025-explained.

2 McBride, James, and Chatzky, Andrew. (2019, May 13). *Is Made in China a Threat to Global Trade?* Background Note, Council on

Foreign Relations, available at: https://www.cfr.org/backgrounder/made-china-2025-threat-global-trade.

3 Incidentally, ACMDs have been inventoried here, and explained here. Singham, Abbott, Rangan and others have written extensively on the subject of ACMDs. More research in this important area needs to be done, encouraged and supported.

4 See Singham, Shanker A., and Sokol, Daniel D. (2004, Summer). Public Sector Restraints: Behind the Border Trade Barriers. *Texas International Law Journal*, available at: Texas International Law Journal; For an early treatment see Singham, Shanker A. (1999). Market Access and Market Contestability: Is the Difference Purely Semantics: A Business Perspective. *Brook. Journal of International Law* 25, available at: https://brooklynworks.brooklaw.edu/bjil/vol25/iss2/24.

5 See Competere-Sample-Chapter-Report-Final.pdf.

6 The Impact of Carbon Leakage mechanisms on Growth, Growth Commission (October 2024) available at: CBAM-final-pdf.pdf.

7 Credible commitments are an essential part of any agreement between parties, be they individuals, businesses or governments. Credible commitments promote trust and cooperation. For an elaboration of the concept and its importance, see North, Douglass C. (1993). Institutions and Credible Commitment. *Journal of Institutional and Theoretical Economics* 149(1), 11–23 and Schelling, Thomas C. (1980). *The Strategy of Conflict*. Cambridge, MA: Harvard University Press.

8 See Singham, Shanker A. (1999). Market Access and Market Contestability: Is the Difference Purely Semantics: A Business Perspective. *Brook. Journal of International Law* 25, available at: https://brooklynworks.brooklaw.edu/bjil/vol25/iss2/24.

9 Brooke Group Ltd. v. Brown & Williamson Tobacco Corp., 509 U.S. 209 (1993); For a more extensive treatment of this topic, see Singham, Shanker A., and Abbott, Alden F. (2023). *Trade, Competition and Domestic Regulatory Policy*. Routledge.

10 OECD See note: 1.

11 OECD, See note 1, For instance, EU member states were required under Article 22 of the EU Postal Services Directive to "designate one or more national regulatory authorities for the postal sector that are legally separate from and operationally independent of the postal operators". Some have integrated such regulator in the competition authority (e.g. Australia, the Netherlands and Spain). These regulatory authorities are also members of the European Regulators Group for Postal Services (ERGP), an advisory group to the EC that facilitates consultation and cooperation and ensures the consistent application of the postal and parcel legislation. This ERGP acknowledges the risks of cross-subsidisation in its report from 2019.2 Notes: 1 Directive 2008/6/EC of the European Parliament and the Council of 20 February 2008 amending Directive 97/67/EC with regard to the full accomplishment of the internal market of Community postal services, https://eur-lex.europa.eu/legalcontent/EN/TXT/?uri=celex:32008L0006. 2 "ERGP Report on the cross-subsidisation", European Regulators Group for Postal Services, 4 October 2019. Sources: (Cohen, 2004[36]);

(Geddes, 2008[37]); (OECD, 1999[38]); OJ C 39, 6.2.1998, Notice from the Commission on the application of the competition rules to the postal sector and on the assessment of certain State measures relating to postal services.

12 European Commission, 20 March 2001, Case 35.141, Deutsche Post AG, [2001] OJ L125/27.

Commission Decision 2001/892/EC of 25 July 2001 Deutsche Post AG L.331/40 15/12/2001.

13 See for example Singham, Shanker A., and Abbott, Alden F. (2023). *Trade, Competition and Domestic Regulatory Policy*. Routledge; Singham, Shanker A. (2007). Trading Up. *The National Interest* 90; Abbott, Alden F., and Singham, Shanker A. (2011). Enhancing Welfare by Attacking Anti-Competitive Market Distortions. *Concurrences* 4; Singham, Shanker A., and Sokol, D. Daniel. (2004, Summer). Public Sector Restraints: Behind the Border Trade Barriers. *Texas International Law Journal*; Singham, Shanker, Rangan, U. Srinivasa, and Bradley, Robert F. (2014). The Effect of Anti-Competitive Market Distortions (ACMDs) on Global Markets. *Law and Economics, Concurrences* 4.

14 An example is in the area of labour. Labour cost advantage is the comparative advantage of developing countries with respect to developed countries, unless the developing country is deliberately deviating from agreed norms (e.g. using prison labour in contravention of international trade rules).

15 See www.growth-commission.com for a series of papers that show how the three different pillar scores impact GDP per capita.

16 See the ACMD model used by the Growth Commission (www.growth-commission.com) drawn from the work of Shanker Singham and Alden Abbott in Footnote 1, and the SRB ACMD model available at: https://shankersingham.com/wp-content/uploads/2023/08/LIACMDIndia.pdf and more generally at www.shankersingham.com.

17 The precise methodology can be found in www.growth-commission.com.

18 For a detailed treatment, see Singham, Shanker A. (2007). A General Theory of Trade and Competition. In *Trade Liberalisation and Competitive Markets*. CMP; and Singham, Shanker A., and Abbott, Alden F. (2023). *Trade, Competition and Domestic Regulatory Policy*. Routledge.

Bibliography

OECD, Subsidies. (2022). *Competition and Trade, OECD Competition Policy Roundtable, Background Note*, available here.

See for example Singham, Shanker A. (1999). Market Access and Market Contestability: Is the Difference Purely Semantics? *Brook. Journal of International Law* 25, 337.

Singham, Shanker A. (2001, Summer). Advancing the Competition and Trade Policy Agenda: Public Sector Restraints on Trade in the Free Trade Area of the Americas. *International Antitrust Bulletin* 4, 2.

Singham, Shanker A., and Sokol, D. Daniel. (2004). Public Sector Restraints; Behind the Border Trade Barriers. *Texas International Law Journal* 39, 625.

Abbott, Alden F., and Singham, Shanker. (2011, November). Enhancing Welfare by Attacking Anticompetitive Market Distortions. *Revue Concurrences* 4, 39547.

See Singham, Shanker A., and Rangan, U. Srinivasa. (2014, December). *The Effect of Anticompetitive Market Distortions (ACMDs) on Global Markets Concurrences*.

See Anti-Competitive Market Distortions and their Impact; A case study of India, Singham, Rangan, Bradley and Kiniry (see here); See also An Introduction to Anti-Competitive Market Distortions, Legatum Institute, September, 2016, available here.

See especially FN 3, 4 and 5.

SeeAn Agent Based model of Trade; Market Distortions and Output, Cebr, 2019, February, available at: https://img1.wsimg.com/blobby/go/bf4d316c-4c0b-4e87–8edb-350f819ee031/downloads/Cebr%20Market%20Distortions%20Trade%20Report.pdf?ver=1603533215968.

Cebr. (2019, October). *An Agent-based Model of Trade: Market Distortions and Output*, available here.

Address by Mr. Rod Sims, Making markets work for increased productivity and growth: the Australian experience address, available here.

Australian Government Productivity Commission. (2005, February 28). *Review of National Competition Policy Reforms: Productivity Commission Inquiry Report*, available here.

Singla, Shikar. (2023, February 23). *Regulatory Costs and Market Power.* LawFin Working Paper No. 47, available here.

Erixon, Frederik, Guinea, Oscar, and du Roy, Oscar. (2023, July). *If the EU was a State in the United States: Comparing Economic Growth between EU and US States*. ECIPE, available here.

See papers available at: Research – Page 2 – The Growth Commission.

These have been introduced in Singham and Abbott, Trade, Competition and Domestic Regulatory Policy as well as the e-resource available at: Further-Refinements-and-Developments-of-ACMD-Economic-Model2.pdf.

As proposed and argued in Singham, Shanker. (2007). *A General Theory of Trade and Competition: Trade Liberalisation and Competitive Markets*. Cameron May, and Singham, Shanker, and Abbott, Alden F. (2023). *Trade, Competition and Domestic Regulatory Policy*. Routledge; International competition is way of describing the openness of a country's trade regime.

Furubotn, Eirik G., and Pejovich, Svetozar. (1972, December). Property Rights and Economic Theory: A Survey of the Recent Literature. *Journal of Economic Literature* 10(4), 1137–1162.

Besley, Timothy. (1995, October). Property Rights and Investment Incentives: Theory and Evidence from Ghana. *The Journal of Political Economy* 103(5), 903–937.

A lack of property rights protection creates what De Soto calls "dead capital" – the poor cannot leverage the assets they do accumulate, which prevents entrepreneurialism. See: Soto, Hernando De. (2000). *The Mystery of Capital: Why Capitalism Triumphs in the West and Fails Everywhere Else*. New York: Basic. Print.

For a detailed treatment of the importance of intellectual property rights, see chapter 9 of: Singham, Shanker. (2007). *A General Theory of Trade and Competition: Trade Liberalisation and Competitive Markets*. Kent: Cameron May.

Either financially or through time commitments.

That is, Heritage Foundation describes why a country receives each level of score and this, in turn, provides a framework for the aspects of policy which we considered in building our indicator, available at: http://www.heritage.org/index/property-rights.

Porter, Michael E. (1990). *The Competitive Advantage of Nations*. New York: Free Press. As cited in Sakakibara, Mariko, and Porter, Michael E. (2001, May). Competing at Home to Win Abroad: Evidence from Japanese Industry. *The Review of Economics and Statistics* 83(2), 310–322. Positive externalities include, ". . . supplier availability, easier access to technology and market information, and specialized human resource development" (Sakakibara et al. p. 310).

As part of our domestic competition indicator, we include an indicator of the success of policy in limiting the ability of private entities to restrict competition through the "Effectiveness of Anti-Monopoly Policy" variable in the "Industrial Organization Regulation" subcategory.

Muris, Timothy J. (2005, Winter). Principles for a Successful Competition Agency. *University of Chicago Law Review* 72(1), 165–187; George Mason Law & Economics Research Paper No. 06–24, available at: SSRN: http://ssrn.com/ abstract=90167.

Similarly, the Washington Consensus includes privatisation as one of the 10 key areas of development because of the belief that that "private industry is managed more efficiently than state enterprises, because of the more direct incentives faced by a manager who either has a direct personal stake in the profits of an enterprise or else is accountable to those who do. At the very least, the threat of bankruptcy places a floor under the inefficiency of private enterprises, whereas many state enterprises seem to have unlimited access to subsidies". This theory is the backbone of our domestic competition indicator. However, regulation of private markets is not discussed in the Washington Consensus. We correct this oversight by emphasising the importance of policies which allow firms to make their own decisions. Originally conceived in: Williamson, John. (1990, April). What Washington Means by Policy Reform. Chapter 2 from *Latin American Adjustment: How Much Has Happened?* Ed. John Williamson, available at: http://iie.com/publications/papers/paper.cfm?ResearchID=486 See also: http://www.who.int/trade/glossary/ story094/en/

http://www.economicshelp.org/blog/7387/economics/washington-consensus-definition-and-criticism/

http: //www.piie.com/publications/chapters_preview/6628/02iie6628.pdf

When changing market characteristics, such as new technologies, eliminate natural monopoly conditions; however, maintaining government regulation may become counterproductive and welfare-inimical, and such regulation should be lifted.

Before the government acts, care should be taken to ensure that the private sector cannot adequately rectify the market failure at issue, and that the costs associated with government intervention are not likely to outweigh the benefits that flow from eliminating (or reducing) the market failure.

The welfare-maximising number and size of firms will depend on the market (type of good, substitutes, demand, etc.).

The ideal infrastructure measures would be those that reflect the policy for awarding contracts for infrastructure projects (specifically, for building, managing or maintaining infrastructure). However, the primary data available are concerned with outcomes, with only a couple of exceptions in financial infrastructure.

For a description of the theory, see: Bajona, Claustre, Gibson, Mark J., Kehoe, Timothy J., and Ruhl, Kim J. (2008). *Trade Liberalization, Growth, and Productivity*. Prepared for the Conference "New Directions in International Trade Theory" at the University of Nottingham, available at:

http://www.econ.umn.edu/~tkehoe/papers/BajonaGibsonKehoeRuhl.pdf.

Note: These authors also highlight the fact that trade openness does not always lead to increased GDP and that the theory does not predict an increase in GDP from openness. The theory does predict greater welfare from openness, though. We will use GDP per capita as our proxy for welfare because we do not have a direct measure of welfare. There are many sources which do find a positive relationship between openness and GDP. A few examples include (as cited in Bajona et al. (2010)): Frankel, J. A., and Romer, D. (1999). Does Trade Cause Growth? *American Economic Review* 89, 379–399. Hall, R., and Jones, C. (1999). Why Do Some Countries Produce So Much More Output Per Worker Than Others? *Quarterly Journal of Economics* 114, 83–116. Alcalá, F., and Ciccone, A. (2004). Trade and Productivity. *Quarterly Journal of Economics* 119, 613–646.

Economics, 119, 613–646. Williamson, John. (1990, April). What Washington Means by Policy Reform. Chapter 2 from *Latin American Adjustment: How Much Has Happened?* Ed. John Williamson, available at: http://iie.com/publications/papers/paper.cfm? ResearchID=486.

Though, again, no emphasis was given to the competitive environment within a country except for the stress on privatisation.

See SRB (2014).

Source: http://unctadstat.unctad.org/wds/ReportFolders/reportFolders.aspx?sRF_ActivePath=p,5&sRF_Expanded=,p,5

Source for health expenditures per cap, domestic credit stock, school persistence, fuel exports, and ore and metal exports: http://databank.worldbank.org/data/home.aspx

Solow, Robert M. (2001). What Have We Learned from a Decade of Empirical Research on Growth? Applying Growth Theory across Countries. *The World Bank Economic Review* 15(2), 283–288, available at: https://doi.org/10.1093/wber/15.2.283.

Economic factors include things like "size of the government", "openness of the economy", etc.; *Institutions* includes things like "political stability", "democratic rights", etc.; *Social base* includes things like "ethnic and religious composition of the population", etc.; *Physical base* includes things like "location of a country", "climate", "access to sea", etc.

Source: Islam, Nazrul. (2005, October). *Determinants of Productivity: A Two-Stage Analysis*. Working Paper Series 2005–13. International Centre for the Study of East Asian Development.

Solow, Robert M. (1956, February). A Contribution to the Theory of Economic Growth. *The Quarterly Journal of Economics* 70(1), 65–94.

Total factor productivity (TFP) has been shown to be a key component of productivity as well (for example: Solow, Robert M. (1957, August). Technical Change and the Aggregate Production Function. *Review of Economics and Statistics* 39, 312–320; Denison, Edward F. (1985). *Trends in American Economic Growth, 1929–1982*. Washington: Brookings Institution; Jones, Charles I. (1997, Summer). On the Evolution of the World Income Distribution. *Journal of Economic Perspectives* 11, 19–36.). TFP is typically measured as the Solow residual, which would be the residual in our model. Our concern here is estimating the effect of removing ACMDs on GDP through the effect of reducing ACMDs on capital and labour. This is essentially the first step in the process of using the ACMD index to evaluate the impact of ACMDs. Future research should attempt to disaggregate the types of inputs (capital, labour, TFP) to find the specific way in which ACMDs reduce productivity and welfare.

Numerous studies show this relationship. A few examples include:

Barro, Robert J. (1991, May). Economic Growth in a Cross Section of Countries. *Quarterly Journal of Economics* 106(2), (May, 1991), pp. 407–443. https://www.jstor.org/stable/2937943

Mauro, Paolo. (1995, August). Corruption and Growth. *Quarterly Journal of Economics*. 110(3) (Aug., 1995), pp. 681–712. https://www.jstor.org/stable/2946696

Besley, Timothy. (1995, October). Property Rights and Investment Incentives: Theory and Evidence from Ghana. *The Journal of Political Economy* 103(5), 903–937.

Svensson, Jakob. (1998). Investment, Property Rights, and Political Stability. *European Economic Review* 42, 1317–1341.

See, for example: Levine, Ross, Loayza, Norman, and Beck, Thorsten. (2000). Financial Intermediation and Growth: Causality and Causes. *Journal of Monetary Economics* 46.

Levine, Ross, and Zervos, Sara. (1998, June). Stock Markets, Banks, and Economic Growth. *The American Economic Review* 88(3) (Jun., 1998), pp. 537–558. https://www.jstor.org/stable/116848

Zagha, Roberto, and Nankani, Gobind T. (eds.). (2005). *Economic Growth in the 1990s: Learning from a Decade of Reform*. Chapter 7. World Bank Publications.

Aiyar, Shekhar, and Jain-Chandra, Sonali. (2012). *The Domestic Credit Supply Response to International Bank Deleveraging: Is Asia Different?* IMF Working Paper WP/12/258. Asia and Pacific Department. IMF.

Williamson, John. (1990, April). "What Washington Means by Policy Reform." Chapter 2 from *Latin American Adjustment: How Much Has Happened?* Ed. John Williamson, available at: http://iie.com/publications/papers/paper.cfm?ResearchID=486.

Adams, Samuel. (2010, July). Intellectual Property Rights, Investment Climate, and FDI in Developing Countries. *International Business Research* 3(3).

Adams (2010) shows that patent protection had a greater, positive influence on FDI after the adoption of TRIPS, which tells us that committing to protecting intellectual property and actually increasing patent protection together attracted more FDI.

Ramamurti, Ravi, and Doh, John P. (2004). Rethinking Foreign Infrastructure Investment in Developing Countries. *Journal of World Business* 39.

Lucas, Jr., Robert E. (1990, May). Why Doesn't Capital Flow from Rich to Poor Countries? *The American Economic Review* 80(2), 92–96.

Bayraktar, Nihal. (2013). Foreign Direct Investment and Investment Climate. *Procedia Economics and Finance* 5, 83–92.

Nnadozie, E., and Njuguna, A. E. (2013). *Investment Climate and Foreign Direct Investment in Africa*. Mimeo, United Nations Economic Commission for Africa.

Pan, Yigang et al. (2014). Firms' FDI Ownership the Influence of Government Ownership and Legislative Connections. *Journal of International Business Studies* 45.

Pilarska, Czeslawa, and Walega, Grzegorz. (2014, September 11–13). Determinants of FDI Inflows to Poland, Czech Republic and Hungary in Context of Integration into European Union. *The 8th International Days of Statistics and Economics, Prague.*

This interdependence has been documented many times. Some examples include:

Dunning, John H. (2003, Fall). The Role of Foreign Direct Investment in Upgrading China's Competitiveness. *Journal of International Business and Economics* 4, pp. 1–13.

United Nations Conference on Trade and Development's World Investment Reports (numerous reports, but the 1998 and 2012 report focus on trends in determinants of FDI and investment climate, political stability and openness of trade are factors in each report).

The literature supports the use of health expenditures as a proxy for health outcomes: Farag, Marwa et al. (2012). Health Expenditures, Health Outcomes and the Role of Good Governance. *International Journal of Health Care Finance and Economics* 13(1), 33–52. Shows that health expenditures reduce child and infant mortality rates in low- and middle-income countries and that good governance improve this effect; Bokhari, Farasat A. S., Gai, Yunwei, and Gottret, Pablo. (2007). Government Health Expenditures and Health Outcomes. *Health Economics* 16(3), 257–273. Shows that health expenditures reduce infant and maternal mortality rates across all income levels; Anyanwu, John C., and Erhijakpor, Andrew E. O. (2007). *Health Expenditures and Health Outcomes in Africa*. Working Paper No. 91. African Development Bank. Shows that the relationship between health expenditures and child and infant mortality rates holds for Africa; Joumard, I., Andre, C., and Nicq, C. (2010). *Health Care Systems: Efficiency and Institutions*. OECD Economics Department Working Papers, No. 769. OECD Publishing, Paris. Shows that 40% of the increase in life expectancy since 1990 for OECD countries can be attributed to increases in health expenditures.

Cockburn, Iain M. (2009). Intellectual Property Rights and Pharmaceuticals: Challenges and Opportunities for Economic Research. *The Economics of Intellectual Property*, Chapter 5, World Intellectual Property Organization, Geneva.

Berndt, Ernst R., Blalock, Nathan, and Cockburn, Iain M. (2011). Diffusion of New Drugs In The Post-TRIPS Era. *International Journal of the Economics of Business* 18(2), 203–224.

Berndt et al. (2011).

Many studies have examined the relationship between education and productivity or wages. Some examples include:

Duflo, Esther. (2001). Schooling and Labor Market Consequences of School Construction in Indonesia: Evidence from an Unusual Policy Experiment. *American Economic Review* 91(4), 795–813.

Rosenzweig, M. (1995). Why Are There Returns to Schooling. *American Economic Review* 85(2), 153–158.

Ashenfelter, Orley, and Krueger, Alan. (1994). Estimates of the Economic Return to Schooling from a New Sample of Twins. *American Economic Review*, 84(5), 1157–1173.

We used this specification to calculate the weights because we were trying to maximise the correlation among the three policy areas and productivity through the factors directly affecting productivity. After the weights were determined, we revisited the model and came to the specification used here.

See Singham (2007) and the following examples:

Khoury, Theodore A., and Peng, Mike W. (2011). Does Institutional Reform of Intellectual Property Rights Lead to More Inbound FDI? Evidence from Latin America and the Caribbean. *Journal of World Business* 46.

Eicher, Theo, and Garcia-Penalosa, Cecilia. (2008). Endogenous Strength of Intellectual Property Rights_ Implications for Economic Development and Growth. *European Economic Review* 52.

Iwaisako, Tatsuro, Tanaka, Hitoshi, and Futagami, Koichi. (2011). A Welfare Analysis of Global Patent Protection in a Model with Endogenous Innovation and Foreign Direct Investment. *European Economic Review* 55.

Tanaka, Hitoshi, and Iwaisako, Tatsuro. (2014). Intellectual Property Rights and Foreign Direct Investment. *European Economic Review* 67.

Park, Walter G., and Ginarte, Juan Carlos. (1997, July). Intellectual Property Rights and Economic Growth. *Contemporary Economic Policy* XV.

Pries, Michael, and Rogerson, Richard. (2005). Hiring Policies, Labor Market Institutions, and Labor Market Flows. *Journal of Political Economy* 113(4).

Alvarez, Fernando, and Veracierto, Marcelo. (1999). Labor-Market Policies in an Equilibrium Search Model. *NBER Macroeconmics Annual* 14. Ed. Ben Bernanke and Julio Rotemberg.

The authors also compare their results with existing empirical studies and find the empirical literature is generally in agreement.

World Economic Forum. (2014). *Global Competitiveness 2014–2015.* Geneva: World Economic Forum.

http://www.heritage.org/index/about.

http://data.worldbank.org/indicator/IC.BUS.EASE.XQ.

The GCI is the only exception because it shifts weights among the broadest categories depending on the income level of the country it is ranking. However, the variables within the subcategories within the "pillars" of these broad categories all have equal weights, as do the subcategories, as do the pillars. The broadest categories relate to the types of production an economy can pursue and the weights are greatest within each income level for the types of production a country at that level of development is most likely to pursue. In this way, the GCI takes equally weighted variables and weights them in such a way as to fit the score of a country to its relative level of income. So, lower income countries will get lower scores and higher income countries will get higher scores by construction.

See, for example: Muris, Timothy J. (2005, Winter). Principles for a Successful Competition Agency. *University of Chicago Law Review* 72(1), 165–187; George Mason Law & Economics Research Paper No. 06–24, available at: SSRN: http://ssrn.com/abstract=901677; Muris, Timothy J. (2003). Looking Forward: The Federal Trade Commission and the Future Development of U.S. Competition Policy. *Columbia Business Law Review* 359, 363.

Williamson, John (1990).

The work on the SRB-γ model refinements was done in collaboration with the Centre for Economics and Business Research, and with Professor Tom Stratmann, George Mason University and Christine McDaniel, Mercatus Center at George Mason University.

Singham, Shanker A., Rangan, U. Srinivasa, and Bradley, Robert F. (2016, September). *Introduction to Anti-Competitive Market Distortions and the Distortions Index*. Legatum Institute, available at: LIIntro-to-ACMDDistortionsIndex.pdf; We also refer to work done by the Centre for Business Research on the development of the SRB model; See also Anticompetitive

Market Distortions: Causes, Consequences and Corrections, for OECD-World Bank Conference, May 2015, Singham, Rangan, and Bradley, available at: Anticompetitive Market Distortions: Causes, Consequences, and Corrections – Draft.

The SRB- γ results section was contributed by our collaborators on this work, Christine McDaniel and Tom Stratmann, of the Mercatus Centre, and George Mason University respectively.

See Posner, Richard A. (1975). The Social Costs of Monopoly and Regulation. *Journal of Political Economy* 83(4), 807–827; See also Tullock, Gordon. (1967, June). The Welfare Costs of Tariffs, Monopolies, and Theft. *Western Economic Journal* 5(3), 224–232.

For an analysis of dynamic systems out of equilibrium, see Prigogine, Ilya, and Stengers, Isabelle. (2017). *Order Out of Chaos: Man's New Dialogue with Nature*. Verso Books.

This work was developed though a collaboration between the author and David Silver, former Director of the Johns Hopkins Applied Physics Laboratory.

CEIC Data. *China PMI: Textile Industry: Employment*, available here.

Note: The end of MFA allowed several new countries such as Bangladesh to leverage their comparative advantage to become major suppliers to the global garment and textile industry, whereas countries like India with its similar advantages lost out due to poor policy interventions.

Source: MeSteel, available here: https://www.mesteel.com/cgi-bin/w3-msql/goto.htm?url=https://www.mesteel.com/info/impo_expo_2011.htm.

See for example Gersten, D., and Caporal, J. (2020). *Trilateral Group Targets China Industrial Subsidies*. CSIS, available at: Trade Trilateral Targets China's Industrial Subsidies.

For a detailed analysis of privatisation in emerging markets, see Singham, Shanker A. (2022). *Market Distortions and Privatisation Processes*. Routledge.

See FN 36.

See Stockman, David. (2014). *The Great Deformation; The Corruption of Capitalism in America*. Public Affairs; Calomiris, Charles, and Haber, Stephen. (2015). *Fragile by Design: The Political Origins of Banking Crises and Scarce Credit*. Princeton Economic History of the Western World; Rajan, Raghuram. (2011). *Fault Lines*. Princeton University Press.

There seems little doubt that the trajectory of EU regulation is in a more anti-competitive direction; See Growth Commission paper 2 for an analysis (available at: GC-Second-Report-The-Impact-of-Regulation-on-Economic-Growth-Sept–2023.pdf); See also Draghi, Mario. *The Future of European Competitiveness*, available at: EU competitiveness: Looking ahead – European Commission.

U.S. Geological Survey. (2024). *Mineral Commodity Summaries 2024*. U.S. Geological Survey, 212p, available at: https://doi.org/10.3133/mcs2024.

Made in China 2025 Explained, A Guide to Understanding China's Next Wave of Innovation, China Innovation Project, Harvard University, Newsletter, available at: https://projects.iq.harvard.edu/innovation/made-china-2025-explained.

McBride, James, and Chatzky, Andrew. (2019, May 13). *Is Made in China a Threat to Global Trade?* Background Note, Council on Foreign Relations, available at: https://www.cfr.org/backgrounder/made-china-2025-threat-global-trade.

Incidentally, ACMDs have been inventoried and explained here. Singham, Abbott, Rangan and others have written extensively on the subject of ACMDs. More research in this important area needs to be done, encouraged and supported.

See Singham, Shanker A., and Sokol, Daniel D. (2004, Summer). Public Sector Restraints: Behind the Border Trade Barriers. *Texas International Law Journal*, available at: Texas International Law Journal; For an early treatment see Singham, Shanker A. (1999). Market Access and Market Contestability: Is the Difference Purely Semantics: A Business Perspective. *Brook. Journal of International Law* 25, available at: https://brooklynworks.brooklaw.edu/bjil/vol25/iss2/24.

See Competere-Sample-Chapter-Report-Final.pdf.

The Impact of Carbon Leakage mechanisms on Growth, Growth Commission (October 2024) available at: CBAM-final-pdf.pdf.

Credible commitments are an essential part of any agreement between parties, be they individuals, businesses or governments. Credible commitments promote trust and cooperation. For an elaboration of the concept and its importance, see North, Douglass C. (1993). Institutions and Credible Commitment. *Journal of Institutional and Theoretical Economics* 149(1), 11–23 and Schelling, Thomas C. (1980). *The Strategy of Conflict*. Cambridge, MA: Harvard University Press.

See Singham, Shanker A. (1999). Market Access and Market Contestability: Is the Difference Purely Semantics: A Business Perspective. *Brook. Journal of International Law* 25, available at: https://brooklynworks.brooklaw.edu/bjil/vol25/iss2/24.

Brooke Group Ltd. v. Brown & Williamson Tobacco Corp., 509 U.S. 209 (1993); For a more extensive treatment of this topic see Singham, Shanker A., and Abbott, Alden F. (2023). *Trade, Competition and Domestic Regulatory Policy*. Routledge.

OECD See note: 1, available here.

OECD, See note 1, For instance, EU member states were required under Article 22 of the EU Postal Services Directive to "designate one or more national regulatory authorities for the postal sector that are legally separate from and operationally independent of the postal operators". Some have integrated such regulator in the competition authority (e.g. Australia, Netherlands and Spain). These regulatory authorities are also members of the European Regulators Group for Postal Services (ERGP), an advisory group to the EC that facilitates consultation and cooperation and ensures the consistent application of the postal and parcel legislation. This ERGP acknowledges the risks of cross-subsidisation in its report from 2019.2 Notes: 1 Directive 2008/6/EC of the European Parliament and the Council of 20 February 2008 amending Directive 97/67/EC with regard to the full accomplishment of the internal market of Community postal services, https://eur-lex.europa.eu/legalcontent/EN/TXT/?uri=celex:32008L0006. 2 "ERGP Report on the cross-subsidisation", European Regulators Group for Postal Services, 4 October 2019. Sources: (Cohen, 2004[36]); (Geddes,

2008[37]); (OECD, 1999[38]); OJ C 39, 6.2.1998, Notice from the Commission on the application of the competition rules to the postal sector and on the assessment of certain State measures relating to postal services.

European Commission, 20 March 2001, Case 35.141, Deutsche Post AG, [2001] OJ L125/27 Commission Decision 2001/892/EC of 25 July 2001 Deutsche Post AG L.331/40 15/12/2001

See, for example, Singham, Shanker A., and Abbott, Alden F. (2023). *Trade, Competition and Domestic Regulatory Policy*. Routledge; Singham, Shanker A. (2007). Trading Up. *The National Interest* 90; Abbott, Alden F., and Singham, Shanker A. (2011). Enhancing Welfare by Attacking Anti-Competitive Market Distortions. *Concurrences* 4; Singham, Shanker A., and Sokol, D. Daniel. (2004, Summer). Public Sector Restraints: Behind the Border Trade Barriers. *Texas International Law Journal*; Singham, Shanker, Rangan, U. Srinivasa, and Bradley, Robert F. (2014). The Effect of Anti-Competitive Market Distortions (ACMDs) on Global Markets. *Law and Economics, Concurrences* 4.

An example is in the area of labour. Labour cost advantage is the comparative advantage of developing countries with respect to developed countries, unless the developing country is deliberately deviating from agreed norms (e.g. using prison labour in contravention of international trade rules).

See www.growth-commission.com for a series of papers that show how the three different pillar scores impact GDP per capita.

See the ACMD model used by the Growth Commission (www.growth-commission.com) drawn from the work of Shanker Singham and Alden Abbott in Footnote 1, and the SRB ACMD model available at: https://shankersingham.com/wp-content/uploads/2023/08/LIACMDIndia.pdf and more generally at www.shankersingham.com.

The precise methodology can be found in www.growth-commission.com.

For a detailed treatment, see Singham, Shanker A. (2007). A General Theory of Trade and Competition. In *Trade Liberalisation and Competitive Markets*. CMP; and Singham, Shanker A., and Abbott, Alden F. (2023). *Trade, Competition and Domestic Regulatory Policy*. Routledge.

Index

Page numbers in *italics* indicate a figure, in **bold** indicate a table and with letter n denotes note number on the corresponding page. Page numbers followed by 'n' refer notes.

FSC
www.fsc.org
MIX
Papier | Fördert
gute Waldnutzung
FSC® C083411

Kolibri 360 GmbH
Ferdinand-Jühlke-Straße 7
99095 Erfurt, Deutschland
produktsicherheit@kolibri360.de